SACRED SECRET SEED

A Love Deferred

SACRED SECRET SEED

A Love Deferred

Dr. Arlene Kearns Dowdy

God's Love in Operation (GLO) Publishing, LLC
920 Haddonfield Road #716
Cherry Hill, NJ 08002

Dr. Arlene Kearns Dowdy

SACRED SECRET SEED, A LOVE DEFERRED
Copyright ©2019 Dr. Arlene Kearns Dowdy, Author. All rights reserved.

No part of this book may be reproduced by any means, graphic, electronic, or mechanical, including photocopying, recording, taping or by any information storage retrieval system without the written permission of the author, except in the case of brief quotations with full citations.

GLO books may be ordered through booksellers or bulk orders may be fulfilled by contacting the author or:
GLO Publishing, http://www.glotutoringandpublishing.org
GLOInc2015@gmail.com
1-609-784-9698

Because of the transitory nature of the Internet, any web addresses or links contained in this book may have changed since publication and may no longer be valid.

All scripture references are taken from the Authorized King James Version, unless otherwise noted.
All images are property of the author or publisher and may not be copied or used without permission from the proper owner.

ISBN: 978-1-734-28211-5 Print Edition

REL036000   REL012050   SOC026010   SCI092000

Printed in the United States of America
GLO Publishing pub date: December 11, 2019

Sacred Secret Seed

To My Baby, My King

Foreword

Any item deemed sacred is valuable to the highest degree. Therefore, the owner of that sacred object often chooses to only show it to certain people or to keep it hidden until certain times or for certain occasions.

Sometimes, when something is easily accessible to everyone, it loses its value. Authentic, natural pearls (the only gem formed in living animals) are extremely rare today. Red beryl, Musgravite, Painite, Alexandrite, and Grandidierite are gems that are way more valuable than diamonds, and they are all so rare that many have never seen their display. They are kept secret and available only to those who cherish, appreciate and can afford their true value. They are not easily accessible.

The most beautiful and expensive jewelry is often only worn for those special occasions. The best clothing and shoes are not worn every day. Otherwise, they will lose their value. In Alaska, there are groups created to watch for and report sightings of the northern lights. The northern lights are a sight of beauty worth watching, and surely, one feels chosen or gifted with the opportunity to behold them. I would think the northern lights would never lose their value, even if one saw them every night of their lives, but of course, they would. They would become a commonality for those people but still, perhaps, of value to those who are not blessed with the opportunity to see them nightly.

Dr. Arlene Kearns Dowdy

The special seed of love that God planted in the hearts of Liston and Arlene the summer of 1978 is of special, sacred value. This seed, although felt by both of them, was planted unknown to either of them. Nevertheless, the life in the seed was definitely at work throughout the years. This valuable and sacred seed, protected and full of promise was germinated only in God's timing. The fruit of the seed could not burst through the surface to be seen by man, until their time was fully come.

This love, the fruit of the seed, was seriously needed by both Liston and Arlene and was extremely valuable to them, yet it remained a secret seed. After a system of roots had been formed all around them, their paths finally came into alignment for the unveiling of this rare and sacred fruit from a seed that had been kept secret for more than 30 years! This sacred, secret seed would develop into the love that always existed for them in seed form but finally manifested visibly.

And the Holy Ghost descended in a bodily shape like a dove upon him, and a voice came from heaven, which said, Thou art my beloved Son; in thee I am well pleased. And Jesus himself began to be about thirty years of age, being (as was supposed) the son of Joseph, which was the son of Heli. (Luke 3:22-23)

What sacred secret seed is growing in you?

Table of Contents

Chapter 1 1
    The seed watered

Chapter 2 7
    Deep roots~divine connections~

Chapter 3 11
    Growing with weeds

Chapter 4 17
    Weeding

Chapter 5 21
    When the seed was planted

Chapter 6 29
    Pruning

Chapter 7 33
    Liston's desire- sprouting

Chapter 8 39
    Freedom-loosed to grow!

Chapter 9 45
    Buds are in view

Chapter 10 51
    A problem solved

Chapter 11 55
    Not, "my friend"

Chapter 12 73
    SEPARATED BY DISASTER

Chapter 13 77
    MAKING PLANS

Chapter 14 83
    TOGETHER AGAIN

Chapter 15 87
    INTRODUCTIONS ~ GRAFTING

Chapter 16 101
    MOTHER & AUNT MAE

Chapter 17 107
    HARVEST TIME!

Chapter 18 121
    ON DISPLAY

Chapter 19 129
    ARUBA!

Chapter 20 133
    THE REVEAL

Chapter 21 137
    GOING HOME

    TIMELINE 147

    WEDDING DOCUMENTS 149

    ABOUT THE AUTHOR 158

Chapter 1
The Seed Watered

Are you from Pinehurst NC?
I think I fell in love with you in the summer of
1978. You knew me by my middle name, Liston
from Newark NJ

My mouth was stretched wide! My eyes stared in wondering disbelief at the computer screen in front of me! My eyes darted excitedly between the message and the adult male's picture that was staring back! Sitting at my computer desk in my apartment on Harvest Bend Lane in Laurel, Maryland on June 29, 2009, I could not fathom the reality of what was happening.

"Liston?? Could it really be Liston?? After all these years?" Question after question flooded my brain, and the shock temporarily suspended any further action on my part.

Finally, my voice and brain made a connection and recovered what they needed for expression. "Oh, my God! ... Oh, my God!! ... OH, MY GOD!!!" The repeated words escaped but with louder volume and more stressed disbelief, as they resonated through the apartment.

Jamala was down on the other end of the hall, and she ran up to know the cause of the commotion. "What's wrong? What is it?"

I turned and stared at her. Reason had not yet kicked in to respond to such questions. "Oh, my God!" I repeated.

"Whaat??" she needed to know.

I turned to stare again at the screen. Again, I looked at her. Slowly, my righteous mind began to slow down, so that my memory could incorporate other vocabulary that I had learned during my many years of school, college and reading. I reminded her of times when I spoke of Liston in the past. She remembered. Then, I just pointed at the screen.

She stood behind me to get a good look at the image. Shocked and excited, too, she asks, "Is that him? Is that Liston?"

"Read what he wrote!"

She read, smiled and looked at me. "What are you gonna do?"

Finally! I needed to *do* something. My faculties were slowly returning. The foolishness of shock was waning away, leaving excitement, disbelief, a sense of adventure, happiness, and did I say disbelief? Thirty-one years had been a long time!

I had wondered about Liston so many times since that summer of '78. I would think of him from time to time when I lived in Anchorage, Alaska from 1993 to 2000. That was during the introduction of a new internet experience that connected us with the world! Yep! AOL: America Online. I remember looking for him, searching his name to see what I would find, to see if I could connect with him. I wondered where he was, how he was. Hey, I even wondered if he was still alive! I could never find any information on him, though, so I just always wondered. Between relationships or in the absence of a relationship, my mind would often drift to the memory of Liston.

I can remember times when I would pray for my husband as if I was already married. I believed that my husband was on this earth somewhere. I didn't know where he was, but I knew he existed. I used to wonder if my husband was being held as a prisoner of war somewhere, and nobody knew where he was; that the United States government had already counted him as dead, and one day, he would suddenly show up. I had all types of stories and scenarios in my head concerning the whereabouts of my husband.

I would pray for God to protect my husband and make him strong; that God would keep him safe and encourage him through whatever he might have been going through. I would pray that my husband would always be obedient to God, so that he wouldn't miss his opportunity to have me, and I wouldn't miss mine to be with him. There were times when I would pray so fervently that I felt a real connection, and that I was sincerely praying for a specific individual who was out there somewhere, espoused to me by God. So, I would pray and wait, waiting for that time when I would know who he was. I had dreamed once of getting married to someone, but I was watching from behind and never saw his face. Can you imagine the turmoil of being so close to him, and just not seeing his face?! I was doomed to wait.

That was about 20 years ago. Now, here was a message, and I was staring at an image from the real human being I knew as "Liston," except on this Facebook Messenger inbox message, the sender's name read, "Clay L. Dowdy."

With my faculties returned, I began to respond to his message, and thus began our text conversations. He was still living in New Jersey! We were so close in proximity, yet still so far away. We began to try to catch up the years.

Liston was just setting up his Facebook account that night because he was trying to round up all his military buddies, and someone told him that he could find "anybody" on Facebook. After creating his account, though, the first person he searched for was "Arlene Kearns." Wow! He was still thinking about me! He had not forgotten through the years either.

When my face and name popped up on his screen, he was "99.9%" sure the woman looking back at him was his "Arlene Kearns," so he sent the inbox message. What a miracle!

To even more demonstrate fate at work, I had joined Facebook only about six weeks before, and I almost did not create the account even then. I had been on My Space, and I wasn't at all interested in another social media account. However, I had moved to Maryland from North Carolina, and my NC family, especially my sister, Linda, and nephew, Samuel, kept having these conversations about information that was familiar only to them, and I felt "out of the loop." They convinced me to join, explaining that My Space was history, and they wanted me to communicate freely with them. They told me if I joined Facebook, we could keep up with each other without paying for phone calls. Of course, that was during the time that cell phone calls and texting was quite expensive, and the cost was based on usage: how often you called, what time of day or night you called, etc. So, I created a Facebook account.

I, too, had looked for Liston on My Space and, again, on Facebook, but he had not yet joined. Since he was going by his first name and middle initial, I would not have found him anyway. Our families and friends called us both by our middle names, the only names we knew of each other, other than last names, and our professional names were our first names, unknown to either of us.

Initially, our communication was not intrusively personal or deep and was quite sporadic. We discussed a little of our present lives, mentioned meeting for lunch or dinner at some point in the future, but both our lives were quite busy. In fact, only a week or so after reuniting through Messenger, I went on a ministry trip to Nigeria for two or three weeks. Then, within five months of returning to

Dr. Arlene Kearns Dowdy

Maryland, by the end of year 2009, I moved out of the apartment and to the Middle East, to Abu Dhabi, to work under contract there for almost two years!

We were so close, but still so far away. However, the seed that was planted in 1978 was now being watered. We just didn't realize that yet.

Chapter 2
Deep Roots
~Divine Connections~

Just as the roots of a seed grow and connect with particles and minerals that give it strength and life, so it was with Liston and me. Roots work and live underground before the plant ever makes its appearance above ground, often forming a webbed system. With me, we were connected through prayer. With Liston, we were connected through his memory of my birthday, December 17th. At the end of the summer of '78, after returning to his new, attic bedroom in Newark, New Jersey, Liston permanently marked my name and birth date onto the wall of his recessed, built-in desk shelf. He wanted to always remember that date.

Shortly after returning to NJ, Liston celebrated his own birthday on August 21st. He turned 12. His mother allowed him to make a long distance call to me for his birthday. That was so special! Long distance phone calls were expensive back then!

Every year until he left his parents' house, he would wish me "Happy Birthday, Arlene," even though I never heard him. After living on his own, until our Facebook Messenger encounter, Liston would whisper or think, "Happy Birthday, Arlene," sometime between December 16th and the 18th. He remembers being on a beach with his army buddies while stationed in California. Somebody mentioned the date, and he whispered, "Happy Birthday, Arlene," even then. He almost missed it that year.

While I was searching for him and praying for my husband—whoever he was, the unsaved Liston was entertaining fantasies wherein I was the star. One of the first songs he introduced to me after we finally started talking was "Fantasy," by Brandi Wells. He said that song always made him think of me.

After Liston and I began to talk more, so many *Twilight Zone* root connections were uncovered:

- During times when I attended St. Paul's Calvary in Union, NJ for church conferences, he was not far away. When I was in Union for other events, like birthday celebrations, he was not far away. In fact, his first cousin, Lucinda, has been a member and a minister under Bishop Campbell for years, and she knew me. She is not just any cousin; she is his first cousin, and they shared an apartment for a few years, while Lucinda and I were in church together from time to time!

- His mother, Palm, and Aunt Dorothy were also going to St. Paul's Calvary.
- One of Liston's best friends and cousin, Little Jimmy, was the son of my mother's first cousin, James Curtis, who used to be my mother's best first cousin when they were young! So, Liston was raised close to one of my mother's favorite cousins!
- Little Jimmy's mother, Chris, and my Uncle Hillian's first wife, Myrtle, are sisters.
- Liston's dad, Cliff Little, is an Eastwood homie, the elder brother of Ricky, whom my Uncle Euland and Aunt Lessie raised.
- Liston and his family know another of my mother's favorite first cousins, Cleo, and her husband, Joe, really well!
- Liston's biological father and his native family are from Carthage, NC, and Mother Ray, from my mother's church, knows and remembers them well.

Divine Providence and timing are all in God's hands. With all those people connections, just naturally speaking, we should not have been separated those 31 years, but then, we would not have this story to tell!

- While I was praying for "my husband," two gunmen walked right in front of Liston and fired shots at the friend with whom Liston was talking. The friend passed out; they all thought he was shot; the gunmen left, but miraculously, his friend had not been shot.

- While I was in Anchorage praying for "my husband," a gang of guys was fighting in a store Liston had stopped in on his way to work; when Liston went to his truck, the guys mistook him for someone else; two cars, one in front of him and one behind him, pulled up and stopped; one shooter started walking toward him and reached inside his coat to pull out a gun, but right at that moment, policemen showed up, and Liston pulled off and got away.

- A few years before I moved to Anchorage, Liston had already traveled there.

~~*~~

You never know what God is doing, until He reveals His work to you. When you trust the love and plan of God, you never have to become anxious. He is working His plan.

Chapter 3
Growing with Weeds

I would not be telling you the full story, if I didn't share the times after the seed was planted and the times after the seed was watered. You would miss some important lessons, if I failed to share the "other times." See, during the growing time, there were storms, famines, droughts, and times when I almost gave up on trusting the promises to be fulfilled.

I had dated several men and even received a couple of informal proposals. Several times, I thought I was with the one who would become my husband, just to realize later that I was not. I decided I did not want to play the dating game anymore, and I informed God about that.

"Lord, please let my next relationship be the permanent one. I'm so tired of going in and out of relationships. I'm tired of getting to know the wrong one, Lord. May I, please, just meet my husband!"

I didn't just date for the sake of "having a man." I only dated when there was a definite connection felt mutually. I dated when I felt that this one could possibly become my husband. Was there another reason to date? So, my relationships were long-lasting and meaningful. The relationship would develop over several years, so when I would realize he wasn't the one, the parting and separation would be heart-breaking. It would take me almost as long to get over that type of breakup, as it did to develop the relationship.

That is the reason I did not want to date for a while. I didn't want to date, until I knew. Well, as the years continued, I changed my mind. I wanted a friend with whom to go places and enjoy special holidays and occasions—especially Valentine's Day and the Christmas holiday. So, I started dating again. My relationships taught me a lot about men, about people in general, about my family, but most importantly, about myself.

During the two years after the seed was watered, in spite of ministry growth, in spite of watching the hand of God in ways I had never known Him, there were times of confusion. Liston wasn't the only one I thought God had brought back to me, but he was the first one. Two other times, I thought "maybe." However, each of those times ended in pain and confusion. And in that pain, those weakest hours, Satan went in for the "kill."

Prophecies had been spoken in and over my life, and they just didn't seem to be being fulfilled. So many situations had the appearance of being right that I was trying to make them right! I was thinking of my age and wondering why God wanted me all to Himself.

I even complained to God once, "Lord, if You want me all to Yourself, why do I need to be here on this earth? Why don't You just take me Home to live with You. Then, I won't have to go through any of this hurt anymore." I remember crying my broken heart out one Christmas morning, after being let down and disappointed, and that just was not like me! How did I get to that place?

However, spiritually, I was in compromise. Had I not been in compromise, I would not have weakened to be tricked or placed in situations to be hurt or to learn what I would rather not have known about some "men of God," or even about myself for that matter.

There were two spiritual disappointments that just left me devastated. There were two young pastor friends, one I had known for years and the other I had not known long. The one I had known the longest lost his righteous mind, and I literally had to fight him off because he was forcing himself on me. I repeatedly had to scream, "This is ME!" I could tell that his mind kept going somewhere other than right there. Something wasn't right at all, and I had to pray. Each time I yelled, "This is ME!" he would stop and apologize pathetically, but the next second, he would try all over again. I became angry, so I had to pray to get away from that situation. I could tell that a show of anger would not end well in this case.

This was a meeting that I did not want to attend with him and kept refusing. He even had the audacity to ask, "How do you know God hasn't given me something to tell you before you get on the road?"

To which I responded, "If that is the case, you can tell me on the phone. You don't need to meet with me." He promised me he would stop harassing me with constant calls, if I just met him. It was broad daylight and in public, so I had no idea he would try what he did. I just wanted to be left alone! I was hurt, confused and both spiritually and naturally angry.

The other pastor, while nowhere near that extreme, tried to use my ministry and the prophetic gift that we had in common as an excuse that I should understand his loneliness. Loneliness? He was married with children! I just told him off and moved on, but my heart was broken to have experienced for myself, not one, but two pastors using their positions to sin, just as Eli's sons did. I was angry that they tried "me," and thought I would fall for it. I didn't understand that, except that I let my guard down. You hear of these things happening but never expect they will happen to you. God wanted me to really "see" and "know," so I would never hurt anyone by simply dismissing them.

I share these incidents because Satan is always on his job, lurking and sometimes, just when you're at the brink of a breakthrough, the night seems darkest, the storms rage more vehemently, and Satan attacks you during your weakest hours of famine.

Continue in prayer and fasting. Pray without ceasing. Don't let your guard down, ever! The prophecies concerning you will be fulfilled! Hold on! Don't quit! Don't give up! Don't even "almost" give up! Be strong! Please.

After all the years of being strong, it was after the watering, when my gift was "right there," that Satan hit me the hardest. During times of hurt, confusion, disappointment and sorrow, he will go for the weak area.

~~*~~

When you "sense" your sister or brother is getting weak in the waiting, please encourage her or him. You don't have to know what's going on. You don't even need to ask questions. Just spend time with her. Pray with her. Have fun with her. Surround her.

I thank God for His Holy Spirit that never leaves us nor forsakes us. My gift was certainly my saving grace.

Dr. Arlene Kearns Dowdy

A "place" of darkness

Chapter 4
Weeding

It was March 2012. I was going to be driving that day from Pinehurst, NC to Augusta, GA to stay with my cousin, Fran, until her husband ended work that year and was able to relocate. She was kind of nervous to stay in a new place alone, but I had lived alone for years, so I was used to it.

Friends and relatives know that I had a habit of falling asleep while driving. Earlier, on the day of my first trip to Augusta, I was trying to get some rest, but Liston and I started texting in Messenger. We had been communicating this way pretty regularly for about three months. I was groggy; without thinking clearly, I requested, "Will you call me while I'm on the road to make sure I'm awake?"

He agreed. "Sure. Just send me your phone number."

OH, NO! Alarmed, I became fully alert! What had I just done?! I had not given him my number before. We had not talked. We had only been texting. Would he think that was forward of me? Is this what I really want to do? Do I tell him, 'Never mind'? What do I do? After more thought, sleepiness returned; I shrugged, gave in and sent him my number and wondered if he would actually call. I continued my rest before time to get up for the drive.

Traveling to Augusta, I was on a back road for about 30 minutes where there was no phone reception. I was not aware when the reception went away, but when the reception returned, I heard the beeps that informed me of missed calls and texts.

He had called! Liston had called and left a message! I was going to hear his voice! Was I ready for this? Excited and nervous at the same time, I clicked the notification to listen. *Oh my goodness!* I was actually listening to Liston Dowdy, after all these years! Wow! What a deep voice! Whoa!

So, I got over the initial giddiness and prepared to return his call. That's when we had our first voice to voice communication and phone conversation in almost 34 years—three years after he had found me again, eight months after my return from the Middle East.

Just before I had left for the Middle East, Liston had greeted me for my birthday on December 17, 2009 through a Facebook inbox. He had done the same in 2010, even though I was in Abu Dhabi. In 2011, I had traveled to New York for a stage play. We were sending more messages by that time. 2011 was the last year he sent a birthday greeting through text only. He finally did not have to whisper it into the air or to a memory.

The phone conversation that day was the first of many. After that, we were on the phone all day long, or at least, it seemed that way: while on the road, even between work and home; while on the job; in the evening and into the night just before going to sleep. We were catching up on all the years and distance between us, until there seemed no distance at all. He even had a tree in this park that he called "Our Tree," because he often parked by that tree while talking to me.

My gift helped me up out of a dark place, out of sorrow and confusion, and I saw in Him the pure, undying, peaceful and sacrificial love of God for me. This was the time of completely getting rid of everything that was hindering the fulfillment of God's plan in my life.

Dr. Arlene Kearns Dowdy

Our Tree

Chapter 5
When the Seed was Planted

As we talked on the phone for hours at a time, we reminisced about that summer of 1978 in Eastwood, NC. We smiled and laughed in the nostalgia of our memories of that special time at ages 11 and 14. We teased each other about one funny memory after another. These were our first conversations in 34 years, so we had a lot to talk about.

I teased him about how he would just sit in a straight chair against the wall in that Eastwood Community Center, staring at and watching me work with the other kids, until I had a moment to look his way. Then, he would just smile, and his eyes, how they sparkled!

My mother, who was the Day Camp Director that summer and was the one who made it possible for us to have the Summer Day Camp, would suggest to me,

"Arlene, why don't you see if he wants to go outside and play ball or race with the boys!"

"I did! He doesn't want to."

"Huh? Humph."

I knew she knew.

Liston was a good kid, a visitor to the neighborhood from Newark, New Jersey. He was spending the week with his cousin, Rhonda Little, in their house right across the road from the center. He was quiet, didn't cause any trouble and just smiled at me all the time. All the kids seemed to like him, and I think every kid in Eastwood was at that camp that summer!

I had been in the car with my mother when she drove to Mrs. Ruth Jackson's house that spring to ask permission to use the building for summer camp for the children. Mrs. Jackson seemed happy with that idea! Then, Mother went through Sandhills Community Action Program (SCAP) to hire responsible youth in the area who needed and wanted to make a little money over the summer. I was one of them, and I helped with directing learning activities, games and crafts inside the building. My cousin, Richard McGoogan "Kent" directed sports and activities outside, and either Evelyn or Virginia Jones worked inside with preparing, distributing and cleaning up after lunch, along with my mother.

Since my mother was a prominent figure in our community—a teacher in public schools, a teacher and leader of youth activities at church, and she had ten children of her own—everyone in the community respected and loved her. All the parents were glad she was going to have a summer camp for kids right in our own neighborhood!

When it was storytelling time, and the kids would all gather around me to hear a story, Liston would bring his chair over from against the wall, and sit near me, too. This was his chance to be as close to me as possible. I think he enjoyed my dramatic reading right along with the others.

In the beginning though, Liston was embarrassed because some girls told me that he liked me, even though anybody would have already known that. He was so embarrassed that he went back to his cousin's home across the street and did not want to return.

When he didn't return the next morning, I asked his cousins, "Where is Liston?"

Smiling in their girly teasing manner, one of them answered, "He's across the street. He's sitting right there on the porch."

Another one chimed in, "He said he's not coming back."

A couple of them were giggling, so as I eyed them, I asked, "Why doesn't he want to come back?"

"He's embarrassed because we told you that he likes you."

"Aww... go tell him I said to come back. He doesn't have to be embarrassed."

They shot across that yard and the street! They were happy and excited to give him that message. I couldn't help but shake my head and laugh at those girls. They were cute and funny!

"Liston! Liston! Arlene said she wants you to come back!"

"She did? She said that?" asked Liston, afraid to believe them.

"Yeh, Stupid, so come on!"

So, Liston returned, confident and satisfied that I must like him, too.

The fact that I was two years and eight months— almost three years— older than he did not matter to me. That, in itself, was a shocker! Even at that age, I never wanted to date any boy younger than me. Now, here was this New Jersey boy, almost three years younger, and he was stealing my heart. See, although he was younger, he was more mature than any of the older boys who had liked me up to that point. He wasn't a "kid," in behavior. He didn't mind showing his obvious loyalty to just be with me or in my presence. He only had eyes for me. He would lock eyes with me, communicating his feelings through his stares and his smile. I had never experienced his level of maturity, except with actual young men who were too old for me, and since I was always mature for my age, I wanted that, and he amazed me being so young.

As we reminisced about that summer, I also teased him about his shorts and long socks to his knees, even in the summer. He confessed to me that he dressed like that, even through high school, until another friend started teasing him!

Initially, he was only supposed to be in Eastwood for one week. Meeting me changed those plans. He called his parents and asked if he could stay all summer. They made sure that was okay with his Aunt Constine and Uncle Ricky.

His dad, Cliff Little, teases him now about that phone conversation.

"Dad," Liston says coolly and in his coming of age voice, "I met a girl."

"What? You met a girl? What's her name?"

They had never talked about girls or anything serious before that short conversation, so Cliff was surprised.

"Arlene Kearns."

"Kearns? Oh! Okay." Being from Eastwood himself, Cliff knew all about the Kearns family, so he wasn't worried about him in the least. He was glad for him that he had "met a girl."

That summer, the popular movie *Grease* with John Travolta and Olivia Newton-John was released. Liston and his relatives went to see the movie, and the characters' situation reminded Liston of our situation because they met during the summer and fell in love, too. The lyrics, "Summer loving had me a blast. Summer loving happened so fast..." and other lyrics were telling Liston's own summer story! After watching the movie, Liston purchased the sound track in a store, and he and his cousin, Rhonda, learned all the lyrics to every song on the album. That was their album for the entire summer!

I remember as the summer camp came to a close either late July or early August, my mom knew that Liston would have to return to New Jersey, so she invited him to have dinner at our house. Nobody seems to remember this event but me. I even remember what side of the table we sat on.

The last day of camp, we exchanged information, so that we could write each other and call, if we ever had the chance. Back then, calling long distance was expensive and cell phones were not even thought of. We probably were just one step up from our former party lines, the ones I explain in *Tales of Eastwood*.

While Liston was in Eastwood, his parents had moved to a new, nice, big home in a new upscale neighborhood. They had given Liston the attic for his bedroom, realizing he was getting older and would need more privacy. One of the first things he did upon being introduced to his new bedroom was to permanently mark my name and birthday into the wooden, recessed, wall shelf of his desk.

Sacred Secret Seed

Liston at Eastwood Community Center 1978

Chapter 6
Pruning

One day, after we had been reminiscing, he revisited his old, attic room in his parents' home, pushed through the dust, furniture and other items that had been stored there through the decades and found where he had written my name and birth date. He took a picture and sent it to me—a nostalgic but romantic moment of many romantic moments.

He also found his old letters from me and started reading them to me over the phone. Wow! What memories they brought back!

He also read the letter that explained why we had stopped communicating. Before this, neither of us could remember why the letters stopped. Well, it was my fault. I had hurt him. I had hurt both of us. I told him that we were "unequally yoked," and that eventually, he would probably meet someone, and I probably would, too, so we might as well stop talking now. I told him I still liked him and always would, but asked him not to send anymore letters.

Now, how did I know that we were unequally yoked? I had not asked him about salvation. I just assumed. At such a young age, I was also afraid of his eventually being untrue to me, being so far away, that I ended the relationship first. That was a move of fear and assumptions, at age 14.

I had totally blacked the memory of that letter out of my mind. I had been playfully accusing him of not coming back to Eastwood to see me, not looking for me and forgetting all about me. After he read the letter, I was the one who had to apologize to him. I'm so glad that God forgives and turns us around, in spite of ourselves, our failures and our mistakes.

On the other hand, my actions could be seen as loyalty to God. I was nearly 15, and I was willing to sacrifice a relationship with someone I really liked and who really liked me to make sure my relationship with God was secure. That makes me think of Abraham willing to sacrifice his son, Isaac. God blessed Abraham's sacrifice, and He also blessed mine.

While spending time together by phone, we were even further away geographically. I had gone further south to Georgia. During this time, I would see and date other friends, but nothing would ever click. I could not figure out why none of the good men who had been in my life were good enough for me to marry! Why couldn't one of them be my husband? I was still trying to remain a certain distance from Liston, not considering him a possibility.

God's timing is so perfect, though. Being with Liston again, even though it was just by phone, was life-saving for me. I was re-focused. My once-scattered mind was now regaining stability. My life was being pruned. I felt happy. I felt in control where I previously had been losing control. God was reeling me in again, and I was allowing Him to. I was still confused about some things, but I realized I did not know what to do with the reins, so I was giving them completely over to God.

I once told Liston, "I think I'm getting too close to you over the phone. We're too far away. I think I need to pull back a little."

Without hesitation, he responded, "We don't need to talk less. We need to talk more."

I secretly thought he was just afraid that I would fill the time we were not talking by talking to other men. I thought that was probably his mannish selfishness, and he wasn't really being considerate of my feelings. I was still trying to keep him at "friend" status. I had some uncertainties and questions, not about him but about the will of God for me. However, I did not pull back. I just flowed with whatever God was going to do.

He would tell me occasionally, "You can talk or spend time with whomever you choose, but no matter who it is, you will never find anyone who has loved you for as long as I have." He would also tell me, "You were the first woman I ever loved."

The guy was deep.

He once sang an entire concert for me over the phone, one song after another, until he actually sang me to sleep! I was feeling badly or sad about something. I don't remember what was going on at the time, but he just wanted me to relax and to rest. He needed to sleep himself, but that night, it was only about what I needed.

After some time, when I thought I was ready to see him face to face, I asked him, "You wanna use Skype to talk?" Again, I was still maintaining "friendship," not relationship.

I really wasn't sure how I would handle seeing him with all the distance still between us, but we were talking all day every day, and I figured we might as well have our conversations face to face—"the next best thing to being there."

His thoughtful and wise answer was "I don't want my first time seeing you, after more than 30 years, to be over Skype. As much as I want to see you, I'm willing to wait for that."

Wow! Okay. Deep and wise! So, we would continue to wait.

~~*~~

God's timing—not ours—is perfect. Trust His timing.

Chapter 7
Liston's Desire - Sprouting

During one of the first discussions we had, Liston shared with me, "For some reason, one of my co-workers gave me a Bible for a gift. I have no idea what made him do that, but I had been wanting to get into a good Bible Study to learn more about God. I just didn't know how or who to go to. I hadn't said anything about this to anybody, so I couldn't believe it when he just gave me a Bible out of the blue."

"God knew, and He used him to let you know that He is with you and that He cares," I told him. "So, have you been studying, then?"

"I've tried, but I think I need a course or something to help me to know how and what to study. I don't know where to start."

So, I gave him some chapters and books to begin. Then, I shared with him a Bible Study website with book and chapter summaries and even quizzes for review after each section. He seemed rejuvenated, and he started his personal study plan.

The next time I traveled to North Carolina, I visited my spiritual mom, Evangelist Ethelrine Hester, and told her all about Liston. I showed her a picture of him, and she was immediately surprised and told me how much he looked like my dad. She was the second person who had told me this. My family did not know, yet, that I was talking to Liston again. I didn't want questions that I was not prepared to answer. I was still trying to hold him at "friend," and I was not ready for my family to be involved, so Mom was the closest family to know about him during this time.

When I shared with her about the Bible conversation, she asked me, "So, is he saved?"

Dude! Wow! Hmm ... *That* should have been one of the first questions I asked him! I guess I still needed some recovery and restoration. The old "me" would have asked him that early on! I was still maintaining "friendship" and not considering "relationship," but still ...

Embarrassingly, I had to admit, "I don't know."

"You don't know?!" both a question and a surprised exclamation of accusation and even more questions all bottled up into one short clause.

Okay! I am already embarrassed! Jesus! How could I not know that already? How could I *not* have asked him that pertinent, foundational question—even for friendship? How could I have been spending so much time with him, albeit over the phone, and not even know if he was protected by the blood of Jesus Christ in salvation? What kind of a "friend" was I?

I was silent. We were both silent for a brief moment. Anybody who knows the two of us knows that silence in our conversations is even less than rare!

"Okay," she continued calmly and resolutely, "you need to find that out the very next time you talk with him, because if he isn't yet, you need to make sure he gives his life to the Lord, or at least, offer him salvation."

"Yeh. I'm going to. I can't believe I haven't. I don't know what I have been thinking. Thank you for that."

Salvation was top priority for our next conversation. "Liston, I know you talked earlier about wanting to know and understand more about God and the Bible, but I never asked you. Have you given your life to Christ? Are you saved?"

"Well, that's what I was trying to tell you. I guess I didn't know how to say it, but that's what I was saying. I want to know God. How do I do that?"

I am called of God to be an evangelist—the first time I ever heard the audible voice of God was when He called me to evangelize! During an early, before-dawn, Sunday morning prayer at St. Ruth United Church of God in West End, North Carolina, after separating myself for a moment, I heard the audible voice of God, and I looked around me to see where the voice was coming from! God had been clearly speaking to me through His Word, the Bible, the previous night, and I knew what I had to do. However, so that I also would know when, God told me, "The time is now."

I don't think I will ever forget that moment, so how did I not hear Liston's heart cry for salvation? Why had I not carried the conversation through to the core and need of his soul? Where had "I" gone? I realized I had allowed too much of my flesh to be present and on the front line, and I was not where I needed to be. I had become too fleshly-minded to be any earthly good. I've heard people use the carnal and sinful scapegoat: "Too spiritually-minded to be any earthly good." That is such a lie and a trick from Satan! The only way you can NOT be any earthly good is to be too earthly and fleshly-minded or "carnally-minded"! There is absolutely no way to truly be too spiritually-minded, Heavenly-connected or God-minded! Don't believe it again. Wash that out of your mind and spirit, and be delivered! Be whole!

God be praised! Liston gave his heart and life to the Lord during that conversation! He finally was able to do what he had wanted to do for some time but didn't know how. This would be the beginning of his ability to understand the Bible and to receive the wisdom and revelation of God.

Maya Angelou once advised, "A woman's heart should be so hidden in God that a man has to seek Him just to find her." Maybe this is true, and Liston could not have found me, until He began to seek God, and when Liston began his search for God, God led him to me. I could, then, help him to know God.

God is so awesome in His doings, and His ways are past finding out, but He reveals His mysteries and His plans to His children.

Dr. Arlene Kearns Dowdy

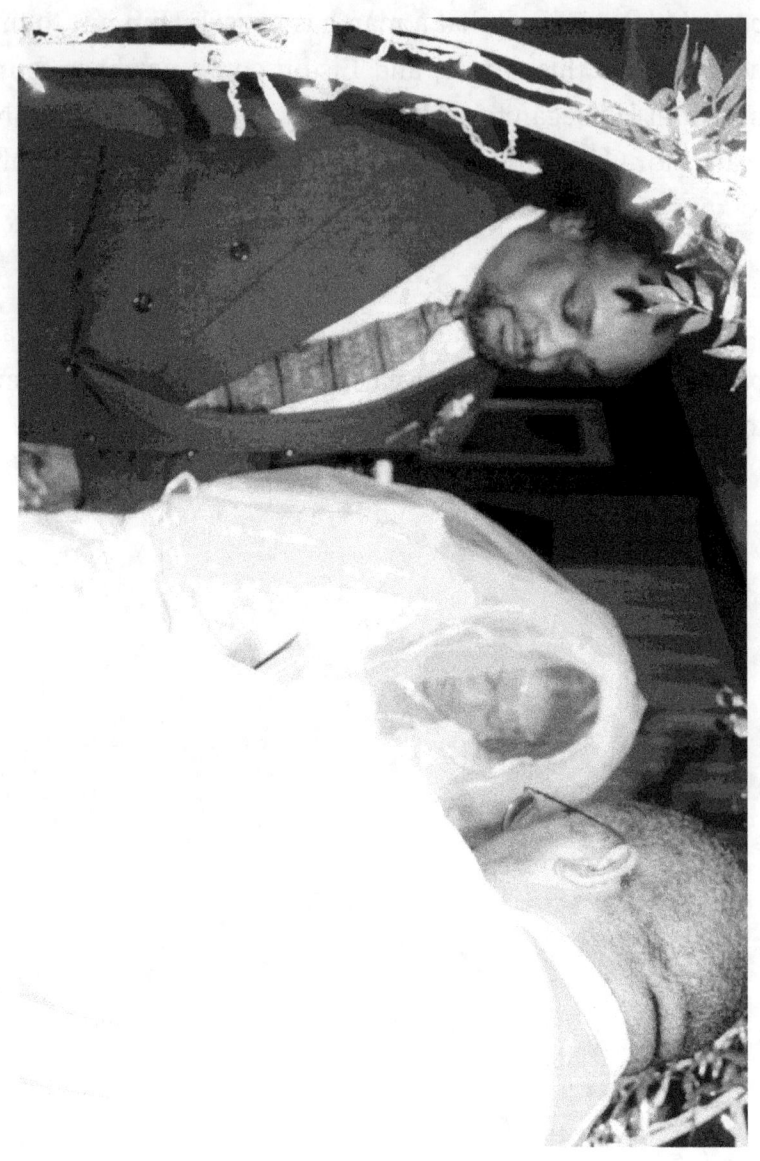

Chapter 8
Freedom – Loosed to Grow!

The 5th weekend in April, I went home to NC again. I had not thought about the upcoming union gathering for the United Church of God. My mother and sister were going to Greensboro, but I decided to stay in Eastwood. I visited a church early that Sunday morning, April 29, 2012. After that service, the day was still young with hours before my mother and sister would return, so while I was driving, I was wondering what other nearby church service I could attend.

While driving, I was talking again with God concerning Liston. I needed to know what to do. I needed to know why he was back in my life. Within two years, I had gone through two similar experiences with a friend from the past suddenly reentering my life, and neither of those men were to be my husband. Although what was happening with

Liston and me was altogether different, I needed to hear from God because my heart was entangled. I had not seen Liston face to face yet, and I wanted to know the will of God before getting even more entangled.

My mind went back to a prophecy I had received maybe ten years earlier, if not more. Apostle Thompson and I were standing on a sidewalk, as I was about to leave after an event. After sharing and asking me to pray seriously with her about a matter, she gave me this look and stated calmly and confidently, "Your husband is coming."

I just looked at her.

She continued to say, "He won't be what you're expecting though. In fact, he may be the opposite of what you've been expecting. He's not going to fit your mold of expectations, so if you want who *God* has for you, you're gonna have to get rid of your expectations."

That prophecy unnerved me a little. My mind is continually working, and I'm always challenged to "figure it out," so I was trying to figure out what would be the opposite of my expectations. My first, alarming thought was, "Lord, I don't want no white man. Please, God!"

I'm not racist, but my desire has always been to marry a black man. That was just my personal preference. I have nothing against who or how anyone else marries. Arlene wants a black husband.

I said to Apostle, "I can't marry a white man."

That put such a large smile of humor across her face that I think she was amused by my fear for a moment.

"I'm not saying who or what he's going to be," she explained. "I don't know. I just know he's going to be different from what you expect. That's all."

Then, I thought, "Is my husband in prison? Is he an ex-prisoner with an awesome testimony?"

See, for years, I imagined my husband would be a preacher. Since I am an evangelist, our ministries would work together. I also imagined that if he wasn't a preacher, he would be a singer and/or musician.

Apostle was observing me intently. She had this knowing and understanding smile, and she sort of laughed at me. She said, "You have to accept the prophecy."

"I don't know," I honestly replied. "I don't want a white husband. I just don't know how I would do that."

She was serious again, and kind of cocked her head. "I'm not saying who or what he will be. He's coming, but he's not going to be according to your expectations. That's all I'm saying." She waited. "You're not gonna accept the prophecy, are you?"

I didn't want to not accept a word from the Lord. I knew that whatever God said would come to pass. I just wasn't ready to *agree* with that one because I didn't know what I would be agreeing to.

"Pray for me," I requested.

That was a lot to grapple with! As I drove away that day, I contemplated the prophecy and had a conversation with God. Eventually, I humbled myself and accepted the Word of the Lord over my life, appended with my request to Him, "Just, please, don't let him be a white man."

The years that followed caused many changes in my expectations and my list of desires. No longer did he need to be a preacher. I had experienced too much for that to continue to be a desired expectation. I don't remember every feature that was on my old list, but I know the expectations changed quite a bit. What I remember, now, is the list that I prayed over in the latter years, always ending with the bottom line of "whoever is best for me according to Your will."

Back to April 29, 2012, and I am in my car once again, talking with God about my husband, but now, our conversation is about a specific man—the purpose for Liston's return to my life. God reminded me of a task that He had instructed me to do a few times before, but I had kept dismissing it. I would receive these soft nudges to ask Liston a question; the answer of which I figured I already knew, which is why I always dismissed the question. I didn't think I wanted to know the real answer. I didn't think I wanted to know the truth that was facing me.

But this time, I declared, "It is what it is." Apparently, I needed to know, so I called Liston immediately and asked him. His answer was not the answer I thought I knew! His answer was favorable! I was overwhelmed with awe and excitement! Now, I knew why God had kept reminding me to ask Liston the question. I was overjoyed! No more walls or abyss between us! I was free to love him! I was finally free! Hallelujah!

While I loudly rejoiced, screamed and praised a while in my newly acknowledged freedom, Liston remained silent. When I calmed down, Liston said, "O-kay... Now, explain to me why that made you so happy. I mean, I'm glad that you're happy, but I want to share in your happiness. Help me understand."

So, I tried to explain everything to him, and what his answer meant for me—for us, and how that answer would change my course of actions.

I had fallen in love all over again with a man who did not meet those earlier expectations but did meet my new expectations and, most importantly, God's desire for me.

When you don't know an answer, and you're dreading finding out what you "think" you know, ask anyway. The truth makes you free. "It is what it is." When God instructs you, don't wait for Him to continually remind you to obey. Act immediately upon His instructions. Your obedience can save you days, weeks and months of sadness, confusion and worry. Your freedom, your victory and your joy are tied to your obedience.

Chapter 9
Buds Are in View

Because I had planned to return to Maryland to live, my possessions were stored in a storage unit there. My brother-in-law, Teddy, and my nephew, Tryston, had traveled from NC and completely filled the unit from corner to corner and bottom to top! However, contrary to my own wishes, God's future plans did not seem to include Maryland for me, so when I went to NC the weekend of April 29th, I rented a storage unit not far from my mother's house and scheduled a recommended interstate mover to move my items to NC. I would have to meet them at my unit in MD. Then, I would have to meet them later in NC or schedule someone to meet them for me at my unit there.

When I told Liston of my plans, he suggested, "Well, why don't I just meet you there?"

Silent screams!

Then, "Oh my God! For real? You're gonna meet me in MD? Really? This is happening?"

We decided to make the most of my visit north and have our face-to-face, long-awaited, in-person, after-almost-34-years, real-live reunion! Even now, a huge sigh just emitted from my body, as if I were still in 2012, seven years ago.

In just a few weeks, I would be able to touch the one I had wondered about and sought for so many years. He would finally be in the actual presence of the "girl of his dreams" and the one he found again. Ahhh! I would finally see, face to face, the man who had found me after 30 years; the man with whom I had only communicated through staggered text messages for more than two years; the man behind the voice that I had been hearing and getting to know for the past two months. I would finally, once again since that summer of 1978, be in the presence of Liston Dowdy. Aye!!

The next few weeks would crawl with anticipation, questions, excitement, fears and so many emotions! All of our conversations surrounded our encounter in one way or another—plans, excitement, nerves, anticipation! My family still knew nothing, so I could only experience this awesome and exciting time with Fran and a few friends. Fran was more like my little sister, though, so I'm sure she had a lot of fun watching me go through this entire journey! She probably heard at least a third of my conversations!

Sacred Secret Seed

The day was Wednesday, May 16, 2012. Two months after that first phone conversation. I hurried to make sure I was on location first, so I could watch him approach. I wanted to see him before he saw me. I thought maybe I could get all my excitement out, before he saw me, so I could conduct myself as a calm and collected black woman.

I did arrive well ahead of him, but he was there before I realized it! I didn't get to see him first! I had been watching from the window regularly, and when he called, I rushed to the window! I had just missed him! He did not call from the parking lot. He was already in the building! Ahhhh!!! Too much excitement! Calm down, Arlene. You've got this. *Can you believe I am feeling those feelings all over again, as I write the story?!*

When he knocked on the door, I had to force breaths and breathe out slowly.

Okay… Okay…

I opened the door.

About four seconds of heart-filled silence followed. Time stood still.

There he was, standing in front of me. All we could do was stand there, smiling. Liston was the first to move. He rushed forward, and suddenly, I was in the midst of these huge arms, embraced in a tight bear hug.

Dr. Arlene Kearns Dowdy

The emotions were so many and so deep that I won't even try to describe them. Those were feelings that could probably only be expressed through some divine music or divine silence.

We shared smiles, laughter, tears. The next few days, whenever I was with him, I seemed to always need to touch him. When we were out eating, I didn't want to sit across from him. I needed to sit beside him, so I could touch him. I don't know if I needed to touch him to make him real; if I was trying to be sure he really had come through that 34-year abyss; if, mentally, I was trying not to let him get away again, or why I had such a need to be beside him always.

He told me, later, that during our reunion, he knew that he could not let me get away again.

We talked so much! You would think that after talking all day every day for the past two months, we would have covered all the topics! We walked around Laurel Lake, which is something I used to love doing when I was living there, but walking with Liston made the walk so much better, more fun and more meaningful. We also visited Dr. Martin Luther King, Jr.'s Memorial and hung out there for a while. Mostly, we just hung together with each other, finally enjoying one another's company in person.

Sacred Secret Seed

May 18, 2012- 2 days into our reunion

Dr. Arlene Kearns Dowdy

Chapter 10
A Problem Solved

After our reunion, we continued to talk all day every day on the phone, but now, we could also Skype: talking, singing and hanging out face to face.

I even met his wonderful, funny and youthful mother, Palm, using Skype. It would be another six months before I met her in person, though.

The next time Liston and I were together, in person, was the very end of June 2012, about six weeks after our reunion. A former UCOG District Sunday School Superintendent, who had been close to our family, passed away in Edgewater Park, NJ. Growing up and as an adult, I had spent time in his house in High Point, NC, and his oldest daughter, Debbie, used to spend a lot of time in my parents' home in Eastwood, NC. I was going to New Jersey for the funeral, and Liston met me there.

Little did we know, then, that we would get married and move to that exact area only one year later. God is simply amazing!

A month after that, July 2012, I moved to Newport News, Virginia where I would be the reading specialist at a high school in Hampton. Yes! I would be closer to him now! It would still be a five to six-hour drive for him to visit, but that was doable, and visit he did, almost immediately!

Dating a saved woman did not come easy to him at first, though. Throughout his life, all he knew was that having sex was the way to show love to your significant other. That was the way he knew to show the other person allegiance or loyalty, to give oneself to another sexually.

We discussed how God's way was just the opposite. We studied what the Word of God said on the subject of fornication. I also shared the reality that anybody and everybody had sex, and that outside of marriage, sex is not really a show of love, but of lust, control, selfishness, greed, comfort and carnality. Very rarely is sex outside of marriage a show of love. I reminded him how the act of sex is used for molestation, abuse and rape, so how can the same act outside of marriage be equated with love?

On the other hand, the willingness to wait, to just love and give of oneself in spirit, heart, and mind without expecting anything in return was of so much more value than giving of one's body in the act of "making love." The wisdom of that truth is not popular, though. I had to learn that, too. We don't always have to make the mistakes. We can learn from the mistakes of others, and we should. I have made plenty of mistakes, but I have also learned from those of others.

Sometimes, abstinence wasn't easy for me either, but I told him I was afraid. I was afraid that the sin of fornication would cause us to curse ourselves and our marriage. I wish I had given Liston the best answer, though. I wish my answer would have been, "I love and respect God too much to displease Him. He has done so much for me that I refuse to serve Satan and my flesh over my Savior." That's what I wish my answer had been, but those are not the words I spoke.

Later, I realized that being abstinent did not seem to be a struggle for him anymore, so I asked him, "You don't seem to be having a hard time now. What changed?"

"Well, I had to change my mind set," was his reply.

"What do you mean, 'change your mind set'?"

"Well, I just had to accept that it wasn't going to happen. Wrap my mind around that and just not even think about it. I just put it out of my mind. It wasn't going to happen, and that was it."

"Wow!" I exclaimed. "That's good! I'm gonna use that to help others who might need it." Ironically, one of the young people had shared with me a similar situation not long before that, and I wasn't sure my counsel to them was enough. This addition would surely be powerful!

Liston's humble response was, "Now, I don't know if that will help anybody else. That's just what I had to do for me."

July 1, 2012 Mt Holly, NJ

Liston's 1st Visit to Newport News, VA August 2, 2012

Chapter 11
Not, "My Friend"

His second or third visit to Newport News was the second week in September. He arrived on a Wednesday evening, and that Thursday, September 13, he was going to take my car to my mechanic for an oil change or something. During a break at work, I called the mechanic to let him know my friend would have my car there by the scheduled time.

When Liston picked me up from work after the appointment, his focused question was, "When you talked to the mechanic, who did you say was bringing your car?"

"You," was my puzzled response.

"Who did you tell him I am?"

"Mmm... my friend."

He gives me this look, which both amuses and confuses me. The mechanic must have mentioned that I told him my friend was bringing my car.

"What?" I asked.

"A friend?"

"What was I supposed to call you?"

"Your *friend*," was the sarcastic, bordering on disgusted comment.

"Well," as I am searching for the best way to explain, "I didn't want to call you my 'boyfriend,' because you're not a 'boy,' and that just seems so elementary and kiddish. I couldn't call you my 'fiancé' because you're not that either. I couldn't say, 'man friend,' because that just sounds too weird. I didn't want to say, 'a friend,' because you're not just a friend. I called you 'my friend' to personalize that you are mine—my special friend. What would you have liked for me to call you?"

Unyielding, he just says, "Not that."

So, I apologized because clearly he was hurt. I just didn't know what I should call him instead, though. I figured I would come up with something that made sense and that, hopefully, he would be okay with.

After making a few stops that I needed to make, he asked if he could make a stop before my next stop. He drove to Jared Jewelers and parked. He collects watches, so I thought maybe he wanted to look at some watches.

We went into the store, and as usual, they greeted us warmly and cheerfully.

"What can we help you find today?"

"I'd like to look at some rings."

WHAAT??????!!!!

My heart and mind are simultaneously clashing, colliding, doing somersaults, totally in hyper mode!

"What are you doing?!" I whisper in alarm.

"Are you looking for a specific type of ring, will that be …?" the sales agent starts to probe.

Liston's looking at me now, like he's won an argument or something, and now, *he* looks amused. "I'd like to look at some engagement rings."

"Ohhh!"

The agent is too romantically excited right now. He doesn't know how unannounced this moment is.

"Well, they are right over here! Do you have any particular type in mind?"

Liston is motioning for me to follow the man, and I am a ball of emotions. I think I am having an anxiety attack, so I am willing myself to pull it together and not embarrass myself in front of this agent and in this store. I feel like all eyes are on me, as each face in the store seems gigantically enlarged with huge smiles on each one. I focus on the agent in front of me.

We start to look in the case at all those beautiful rings! I've never liked big jewelry, not even watches. I like small and dainty. I'm still silently watching.

Liston says, "I think I should just let her choose."

The man says, "Okay!" and he turns his attention totally to me.

"Tell him what you like," Liston prods.

Now, I have to pull in my memory as well as my mentality and cool. Dang! Isn't "he" supposed to choose and just surprise me with it? Why is he having me to choose? How am I supposed to know how much money he wants to spend? Lord, help me! Liston, what are you doing??!!

Then, he comes to my rescue. He can tell by my silence and stillness that something's not right. I'm not a quiet person. I'm not still. That's not my personality.

He attempts to explain, "I just want to get some ideas. I want to see what you like. Just pick two or three, so I'll have an idea."

I look at him, sigh, and start to ask for different rings to try on. I already know the type I like, so I focus on those rings. I try on a few that the agent also suggests, just to see, but I am settling on two or three that I like more than the others.

While I am searching and trying on rings, the agent occasionally looks above me or behind me, and I know that he and Liston are communicating secretly in the way of a buyer and seller, but I am too nervous to look at Liston. I am too afraid to follow the glances, afraid that I will know what is being communicated, and as much as I want to know, I am not ready. I am not prepared!

So, when I have chosen, and I think it is time to go, the agent announces, "Okay! Well done! These are gorgeous choices, and now, the gentleman and I have some business to take care of. Why don't you wait right over here!"

"Over here," is an area I had never realized was there! It was a slightly raised platform, enclosed within a smooth curtain, top to bottom. There were chairs within and bottles of water. No one was in there. I would have to sit in there alone. So, I entered, but not without giving Liston a questioning and accusing glance-- a glance that I hoped said to him, "I thought you said you just wanted to get some ideas. What is happening, Liston? What is going on? Please, help me!"

He just gave me a wink and a smile. So much for the eye talk.

I was alone in this makeshift anticipation lounge. This exciting, nerve-racking yet emotional moment was happening, and I couldn't contact family because none of them even knew I was dating anyone. I didn't want their input in yet another temporary relationship. I didn't want any opinions, yet I knew I would get them, unsolicited. So, they knew nothing, and I was a bundle of nerves, emotions and alone! I contacted two or three friends. I remember contacting Nancy and Debbie through text messages.

"I am sitting in Jared's Jewelry store, while Liston is talking to a sales agent. I think he's buying a ring!! I think he's planning to propose tonight, and I am a bundle of nerves and emotions! I am so nervous, I'm shaking!"

They shared in my excitement, and it helped so much to have someone with whom to communicate in that moment. I certainly needed them!

Finally! Liston came to retrieve me from the anticipation lounge. Whew! I don't even know how long I was in there waiting.

"Let's go," he offered, and I was more than happy to follow.

I noticed he didn't have a bag in his hand. He wasn't wearing a jacket, and I didn't see any bulges as evidence that he purchased anything. As nervous as I was, I was a little disappointed, but I was more relieved. Now, I had time to start preparing myself, since I knew where he was headed. I could relax now and breathe freely again.

"What was that about?" I softly demanded.

"I told you," he said. "I just wanted to get some ideas."

"If that's all you wanted, why did y'all have to talk for so long?"

"Man business. Where do you want to eat?" He changed the subject.

So, now, I knew his plans for real. I mean, deep inside, I knew his intentions. I just didn't expect them so soon.

One of my favorite restaurants, at that time, was located between my job and my home, Joe's Crab Shack at the James River fishing pier in Newport News. My, my, my, did I love the fresh fish and shrimp in that place! Liston would always get this big bowl or bucket full of a variety of seafood with crab legs, crabs and other seafood, along with corn, potatoes and other food items. That was our spot back then!

We enjoyed our dinner that night in a different way. Our relationship had gone a step further, and I realized my life would soon be changing. I was 49 years old. For me, that was surreal.

Liston wasn't the first to have gone that far. I had been led to the jewelry store decades before in pretty much the same manner, suddenly looking at and selecting rings, but this time was different. This time, I knew that change was definitely on the horizon.

We enjoyed the evening and returned to my place. As I walked to my room to put away my bags, I already felt like a different person. My mind is always either reminiscing or imagining, and of course, this time I was reminiscing on the events and feelings at that jewelry store. Those rings were beautiful! I couldn't help but wonder which ring he would choose or had chosen, and when he would actually formally propose. My birthday was coming soon, December 17th, and of course, Christmas was right after. So, I guess I was reminiscing and imagining, too, imagining the perfect proposal, the perfect birthday, the perfect Christmas. You know how a woman's mind works, especially a woman in love who has just been in Jared's selecting engagement rings! What?!

Before I left my room to go back to Liston who was waiting in the living room, I tried to quickly wipe away my thoughts, so I could just enjoy the present time. That was so hard to do, but I knew I would manage.

I got it together and went back to Liston. I didn't want him to wonder what was taking me so long.

I was not one to show a lot of affection in public, so before I sat down, Liston arose and embraced me. We had not embraced after the Jared's episode. We had only stared at each other across the table, taking pictures of each other, both of us knowing, now. An unusual shyness had taken over me. That whole ordeal had humbled me and "broken" my spirit. Okay. I'm laughing now, but "Arlene" was in a different place in her life for sure.

While still holding me but looking into my eyes, he began to tell me, again, how much I meant to him and how thankful he was that God had brought us back together.

"You're the first woman I have ever loved, and I want you to be the last woman I ever love. I want to spend the rest of my life with you." AND HE SMOOTHLY KNELT DOWN TO ONE KNEE WHILE HOLDING OUT THIS BEAUTIFUL RING IN A BEAUTIFUL BOX!!!!!! "Arlene Kearns, will you, please, do me the favor of becoming my wife and spending the rest of your life with me?"

My mouth, eyes, heart and my entire being were gaped wide with surprise! Now, returns that whole flood of emotions! There was no nervousness this time, though, just feelings of disbelief, love, honor, joy, happiness, praise, triumph, exhilaration, peace and so much more! I stared for a moment, until I realized I couldn't keep staring. This man had asked me an important and very serious question, and I couldn't just leave him waiting! I started smiling. Then, the smiles turned to laughter, and I screamed!

"Yes! Yes! Oh, my God! Yes, I will!!"

Again, I don't have the words to express the feelings of those moments. He played the song, "So Amazing," written by Luther Vandross, and held me, as we swayed to the music. He sang these words along with Luther:

> *Love has truly been good to me.*
> *Not even one sad day or minute*
> *have I had since you've come my way.*

Sacred Secret Seed

*I hope you know,
I'd gladly go
anywhere you'd take me.*

It's so amazing to be loved. I'd follow you to the moon in the sky above…

*Got to tell you how you thrill me.
I'm happy as I can be.
You have come, and it's changed
my whole world.
Bye-bye sadness, hello mellow.
What a wonderful day!*

It's so amazing to be loved. I'd follow you to the moon in the sky above…

*And it's so amazing, amazing!
I could stay forever, forever!
Here in love and, no, leave you never,
'cause we've got amazing love.*

*Truly it's amazing, amazing.
Love brought us together, together.
I will leave you never and never.
I guess we've got amazing love.*

*Ooh, so amazing, and I've been
waiting for a love like you.*

It's so amazing to be loved. I'd follow you to the moon in the sky above…

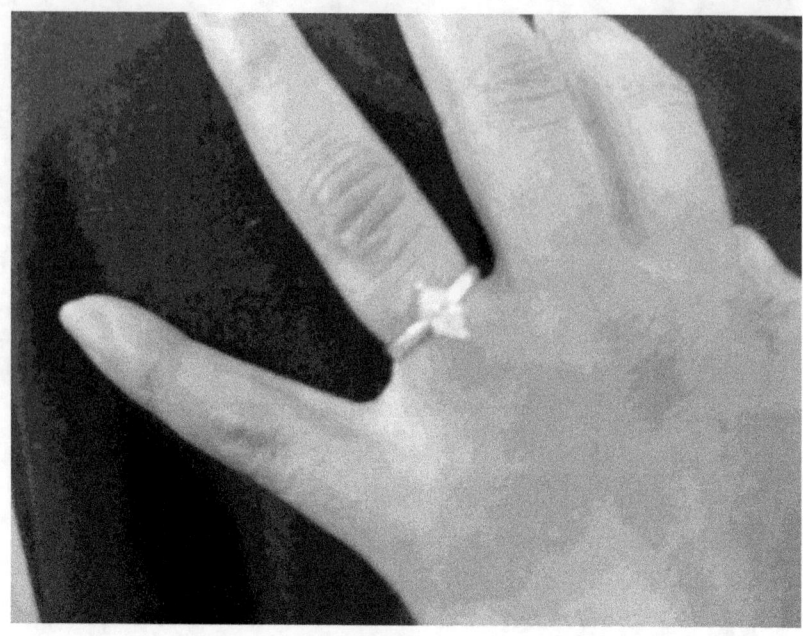

Sometime after the moment had passed, I asked him, "How did you hide this? Where did you hide it?"

"I just took it out to the car and put it in the glove compartment, before I came and got you."

Wow! That had never even crossed my mind!

"Now," he continued, "you don't ever have to tell anyone else that I'm your 'friend'. I knew I had to do something about that."

Laughing, I teased, "Oh! That's why you proposed?"

"Come on," he reasoned. "You knew it was coming. I just decided to do it a little earlier than I had planned. I can't have you going around telling people I'm your 'friend'."

"I love you, Baby."

"Humph. I love you, too, Sweetness."

The next day was Friday, but of course, I did not go to work, and we spent the day out and about taking our own engagement photos. Since the engagement wasn't planned, there was no photographer hired, so we did our own photo shoot. We definitely had to capture those moments!

September 13, 2012 – Engaged!

Sept 14, 2012 - The Day After

Now, it was time to involve my family. I called my mother to tell her about my engagement. Then, I let the other members of my family know. Imagine their shock and bewilderment! They were completely floored! Anyone who knows my mother well, knows that now, the gate was opened wide for her flood of questions!

"What? Engaged?! Lene?! Come on! Engaged? To who? I didn't even know you were talking to anyone! When...? How long have you been talking to him? Did you already know him? Is it anybody I know?"

Laughing at her buzz of excitement, I responded, "You met him years ago, when we were kids. Do you remember Liston Dowdy who attended our community center that summer and didn't want to do anything but stare and smile at me?"

With all the emotions she was experiencing at that time, her old memories were vague, and she could not place him.

"Dowdy? Is he from Eastwood?"

"No. He was there visiting relatives that summer."

"Hmm... I don't remember. I can't place him."

"Okay, Mom, don't worry about it. You will meet him soon, and we can talk all about it."

"Well, how long have you been talking to him? You done gone and got engaged, and we haven't even seen him!" I could tell she was equally as excited as concerned.

"We've been talking for several months now."

"Several months? How many months?"

"Almost seven."

Suddenly, she started remembering details. Oh, Lord! "Wait a minute, now. Didn't Margaret Little's grandson come down one summer? Is it Margaret Little's grandson?"

Wow! My mom must have selected memory. She reached way back into 34 years ago to remember that?!

"Mom, please, just wait and let us give you all the details when you are face to face with him."

"Just tell me if he's related to Margaret."

"Maybe."

"Um-hm. Lord! You're engaged, and we don't know nothing about him."

"You know more than you think, but you'll see. Okay, Mom, I love you! I'm gonna go now."

How about after our conversation, my mother called Miss Margaret and asked her if she had a grandson named Liston Dowdy!! She was determined to go after that information and to find out all she could about the man who was planning to marry her baby girl! She wasn't playing! The funny thing was that Miss Margaret had not seen Liston since he left that summer, 34 years ago, and had forgotten all about him! So, there wasn't much she could tell Mother except, "I think I remember hearing ..." and "You know, I'm not sure, but ..." That was funny to me, when my mother told me! My mother is hilarious!

My brother, Sammy, recognized Liston's picture right away and sent me a text that said, "Liston???"

I smiled that he, too, remembered him after all these years.

Of course, other members of the family also called and had conversations. They were excited, bewildered, anxious to meet him, and filled with mixed emotions.

When Liston told his parents and family, their reactions were pretty much the same, but they remembered "the girl he fell in love with that summer." His dad remembered more about the time because he, himself, was from Eastwood and knew my family. They were all just as anxious to meet me, as my family was anxious to meet Liston.

"So," I began my question to Liston, "do you have any preference for when you would like to get married?"

"As soon as we can."

"Okay. So, let's start preparing ourselves, then. Let's take care of everything we need to do, and we can pray about a date."

Liston's next visit was a month later in the middle of October. We continued to enjoy each other's company and the entertainment and beauty that Virginia had to offer, as we also discussed desires and plans for marriage and a life together. He informed me that not only am I the first woman he has ever loved. I am also the only woman he has ever proposed to. After all these years…! Our discussions, our time together and our love life just kept getting more and more special!

When Liston returned to Jersey that Saturday, we had no idea about the soon-coming disaster.

Chapter 12
Separated by Disaster

On October 29, 2012, just days after Liston returned home, the strongest, deadliest and most destructive hurricane of the Atlantic hurricane 2012 season made landfall in New Jersey, "Hurricane Sandy." Thirty-seven people in New Jersey were killed because of that hurricane. More than 346,000 homes were either destroyed or damaged, and more than two million households lost power. People could not work, because their jobs were destroyed or damaged. They were displaced because their homes were gone. Gas had to be rationed, and lines of vehicles waiting for gas could be miles long, and often after waiting for hours, the gas would be depleted before they could get to the pumps. They started a system wherein certain cars could get gas on specific days to reduce the length of lines and wait time for gas.

Dr. Arlene Kearns Dowdy

For the first time ever, Liston was told not to go in to work because his tower was completely destroyed. Trains and tracks had been horrifically damaged; they did not know when the trains would be able to run again.

This was the fifth most-costly hurricane in U.S. history with the damage and losses set at $68.7 billion dollars! Some of the coastal areas and businesses would never be the same again! Some would never "be" again. It has been seven years now, and while traveling around New Jersey, one can still see the effects of Hurricane Sandy: boarded-up businesses, vacant spots, restructured boardwalks, walled beach lines, buildings that are still unrestored, missing or changed sculptures and iconic monuments, and so much more.

For the first time in 27 years, the New York Stock Exchange was closed down! In New Jersey, many schools were still closed even two weeks after the hurricane hit. Some of the schools that returned after more than one week, had no electricity or heat, so parents were told to dress their children warmly; they had half days, because they could not feed the children lunch. Even with the schools reopening, though, some of the children could not attend because of the housing and shelter issues.

I was so thankful that Liston and his family were all fine. Many were out of electricity, but they were okay; their houses were intact, although some had minor damage.

Sacred Secret Seed

He continued to share pictures and describe life after Sandy. It was like a nightmare. There were so many disastrous stories, but I was so thankful to God for protecting my fiancé and his family.

Thus, our first real test in our relationship came shortly after our engagement. Because of Sandy, we knew that we would not see each other for some time. Even after the residents would finally be able to travel freely, Liston's leadership position on his job would require his full attention and presence for a long time to come. I thank God for His perfect timing to provide our face-to-face reunion before Sandy. During Sandy, we were thanking God for Skype!

Emails during Hurricane Sandy

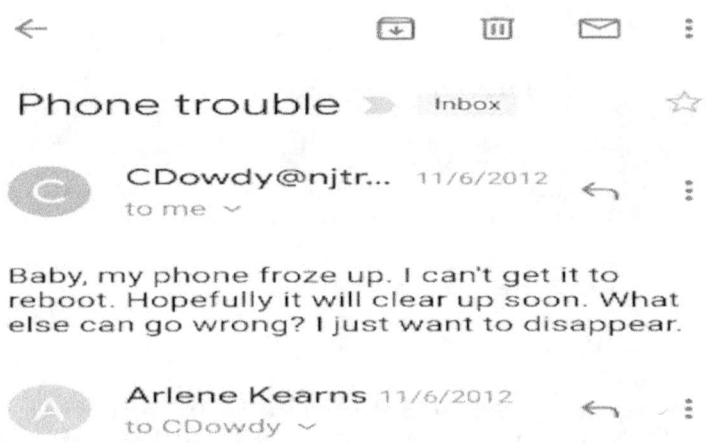

Dr. Arlene Kearns Dowdy

Chapter 13
Making Plans

Three months before Hurricane Sandy, while we were in New Jersey for the funeral, Debbie, was reminiscing about Bishop O.C. Crone, one of our former United Church of God bishops and her grandfather. She remembered that he would always say there was no need for long engagements and tempting yourself, if you know this is the one. Secretly, I did not think she just happened to mention this. I thought she was intentionally using Bishop's wisdom to send me a message. Now, those words kept playing back in my head.

The plans for my wedding had been drafted decades ago, with updates added as needed throughout the years. I knew I wanted a big church wedding, and since I had waited to be married this long, I was determined to realize my wedding dreams and plans.

The question I had to answer for myself was if I wanted a winter wedding or to wait almost a year until the spring or summer returned. The words, "Ain't no need for no long engagements," kept getting louder and louder.

Christmas has always been my favorite holiday because it is the jolliest and most beautiful. I also think it is a romantic holiday and feel that everybody needs somebody at Christmastime.

I have never seen the spirit of Christmas so grand as when I visited "Christmas on the Potomac" in Maryland! When Gaylord National Harbor in Maryland debuted its "Christmas on the Potomac" in November of 2009, the same year that Liston sent me that first, shocking, awe-filled message of destiny, Gaylord National offered local educators nice discounts to spend nights in their resort. When I first stepped into that resort, I was instantly transported to an imaginary Christmas! I don't think I had ever before seen such a spell-binding, elegant and fun display of Christmas splendor! The further I strolled, the more glorious the beauty and wonder of Christmas became.

In 2010, on winter break from Abu Dhabi, United Arab Emirates (UAE), I again visited the Gaylord. Then, in 2011, although I did not stay overnight, I took my first cousin to also experience the glory inside that resort. How I love "Christmas on the Potomac"!

So, I had a conversation with Liston. I did not want to dismiss the wisdom of our former bishop by prolonging my marriage to Liston, but I also wanted my dream. I had worked hard. God had blessed me, through the years, to have the finances, so that I did not need to ask anyone for financial help at all. I wanted the dream.

"Liston, I have always wanted a big wedding. I know all you're concerned with is that we be married, but I want the wedding. I want what I have dreamed about and planned for decades. If I arrange for us to have a simple and private marriage ceremony in December, will you agree that I can still have my wedding between April and May?"

"December? Yeh! Whatever you want, Sweetness. Do you think you can you arrange it by December?"

"I can try. I want to rent a suite at Gaylord National in Maryland and have the ceremony Christmas night after people have already spent time with their families, and they're free."

"Wow! Okay!" he responded.

"Do you think you will be ready by December?" I asked him.

"I'm definitely going to do all I can."

"Okay, then. I'll start making contacts and see what we can do!"

"Hey, Sweetness…"

"Hmm?"

"You're gonna be my wife. I'm gonna marry Arlene Kearns. Some people just sing the song. Some people dream their whole life long, but I can truly say that I'm about to marry the girl of my dreams. Wow!"

"I love you, Baby."

"I love you, too, Sweetness."

"I'm getting married!!!" I thought to myself. Wow! How long had I waited for this day, just to be able to know and to say these words?!

We asked both Pastor Sean, my Abu Dhabi pastor, and my spiritual dad, Evangelist Perry Hester, to perform the ceremony for our big, public wedding later in the spring. We, also, shared with them the plans of our upcoming, intimate wedding ceremony in December, so they would know that at the time of our April vows, we would have already made the vows in December. Therefore, these vows would be an extra seal, for we would be making our vows again to each other, but not for the first time. We wanted them to know, so they would be careful to say, "We introduce *to you* for the first time…"

We asked Pastor Sean, who was still in Abu Dhabi at the time, to be our marriage counselor. Living under his tutelage in Abu Dhabi, I had listened to his teachings on marriage, and his family workshops were amazingly thorough. His own marriage has been such an example, and their testimony of how they became one is also powerful. I knew I wanted his counsel to lead us into our marriage.

Sacred Secret Seed

Pastor Sean consented and wonderfully counseled us through Skype, attachments and email with such meaningful and powerful lessons and activities.

Emails from Liston during Hurricane Sandy

CDowdy@njt... 11/11/2012
to me, claydowdy2010

Arlene, I love you so much more than I could ever tell you.

I have and will continue to desire a life with you. I have wanted to be with you since the day that first layed eyes on you. In all of the things that I have done, and all of the places that I have ever been, you are the one thing that remained in my heart and mind every since that first day I saw you.

I believe in my heart that it is Gods will for us to be together and I pray every day for him to guide us, and bless our union. I ask him every day to give me all that I need to be the best that I can for you. I tell him that my lifes mission is to make you happy and to please provide me with what ever I need to make you happy. I have never prayed the way that I pray now that I have been with you.

Dr. Arlene Kearns Dowdy

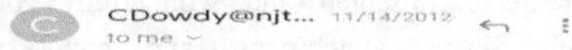
CDowdy@njt... 11/14/2012
to me

Good Morning to the love of my life.
Arlene, you are the one that I wake up to every morning, go to sleep with every night, and pray to be happy with for the rest of my life.
I've spent my life wanting to be with you. Through out my life, I have always thought about you and wanted to be with you. I have lived
A different life from you Arlene and I have done a lot of things. I'm done with that now. Now I just want to live a clean life,
be with you, and get closer to God.

Arlene and I don't want anything more than to be with you and make you happy and for us to be happy together. I want us to get stronger
And stronger together. My love for you goes deep and I want to always work on our relationship/marriage to keep it in tact.

You are my entire world Arlene, I like to be free and open with my love for you. The only thing I love more than telling you what's
On my heart, is hearing what's on yours. When you speak to me and tell me how you feel, I can feel you all through my body. It's a
Feeling that I love to feel. I absolutely LOVE it when I hear you exhale because I know exactly what that feeling is when you do that.
I'm so anxious about you being my wife. I'm so excited when I talk to my parents about you. I love when they approach me to talk about you
Because it give me an opportunity to just talk. You know how I am, I don't like to talk that much but I LOVE talking about you.

You are the best thing to ever happen in my life. You have been a dream for so long that it still feels like I might wake up from this.
I just can't believe that this is happening. I just want you to know that I am looking forward to spending my life with you and that I am
Completely in love with you. Thank God you're here, I love you so much.

You and this relationship are the
Most important thing in my life and I don't want to ever lose this love.

Chapter 14
Together Again

I don't think Liston and I were in each other's company again until the first week in December. Nearly three months had passed since our engagement! Those months had been busy months, though! The plans were made; everything was in place; we were going to be married in a private, intimate ceremony Christmas night, 2012, at the magnificent Gaylord National Resort, right in the middle of their "Christmas on the Potomac"! Plans were also underway for the public wedding the following April. It was a busy but totally happy time for me!

As it was late fall, my yard was filled with leaves, but I was still within the window for foliage pick-up on my street. I would have already gathered the leaves, but Liston wanted me to wait until he could get there. I wanted to help him because gathering leaves always reminded me of my childhood days in the yard with Mother and my siblings. As long as I was working along with a loved one, gathering leaves was fun!

We gathered leaves, put them in bags, shot a few pictures and had a lot of fun! I found out just how afraid of snakes Liston really is! I saw a miniature, white, baby snake. At first, I wasn't sure if it was a snake or a worm. It was so tiny. I wasn't sure, until it began to move. He moved like a snake, so he was a snake! When I told Liston, I thought he was going to just take his shovel and kill it before it got away. My goodness! Liston was the one getting away! So, I killed it. I screamed in laughter because he did not even want to see it. He finally looked at it and realized just how tiny it was.

"Well, see, I knew if it was a baby, the mother must not be far away, so I wasn't running to get away from the baby. I was getting away from the mother. See..." That was his explanation.

The thing is, though, we never ever saw the mother or any other snake after that. That could be because I did go and get a box of moth balls, and we spread them around the outside of the house and porch, praying all the while.

Mr. Dowdy began to seem like a husband already. I was amazed and impressed that he washed the dishes, cleaned the kitchen, and would even tidy the house.

"While I'm here, I don't have to go to work," he reasoned. "You're working, and you're cooking. I don't have anything else to do, so why not help you?" I like his way of thinking. What a man!

Because of the amount of time he had put in at work during the Hurricane Sandy crisis, and because he needed to take several extra days off before the end of the fiscal year, he would not have to go back to work for the rest of December—a whole month! When I say God was working all of this together, I mean there was no way that we could have worked every situation out so smoothly ourselves! We had so many upcoming events, even leading up to our wedding! The fact that he would be off and not have to keep traveling up and down the road alone was only God's doing.

That Sunday, December 9th, my sister Lorraine had passes for us to go to "Christmas Town" at Busch Gardens, Williamsburg to see *"one of the largest Christmas light displays in North America,"* according to their website. Meeting him that weekend, I think she was the first of my "homies" to meet Liston. Christmas Town was beautiful, and we had so much fun walking through that amusement park, recording videos, snapping pictures, eating and drinking hot chocolate! How I love the beauty of Christmas lights, the music, and the happiness and joy that so many share during this time of year!

Christmas Town at Busch Gardens Dec 2012

Chapter 15
Introductions ~ Grafting

After that spectacular outing at Busch Gardens, the next two of our upcoming engagements surrounded the fact that I would be turning 50 years old on the 17th, just days away! My goddaughters had been busily planning a 50th birthday celebration for me, and we were excitedly and nervously looking forward to it! That would be Liston's debut into my family, as that would be our first trip to NC since our coming together and engagement. None of them had any idea that, in just a few days, I would be marrying someone they did not even know—for most of them, someone they had never laid eyes upon. Take a guess at how many family members were talking more about meeting this man who was about to marry Arlene than about my turning 50.

Actually, my first birthday celebration for that year happened a week before my NC birthday dinner! Liston had informed me that his family—this is so wonderfully sweet—his family wanted to throw me a birthday party at his parents' home in honor of my birthday, so they all could meet me! Sister, aunts, uncle, cousins and nephews would be there! I, finally, would meet his family, even before he met mine.

So, Saturday, December 15, I finally met Palm and Cliff, Liston's parents; his sister, Niecie; his aunts, Rabbit and Dot (and Mary, "adopted aunt"); his uncle, "Li'l Boy"; his cousins, nephews and a niece. Liston had talked so much about each one that I felt I knew them already! He had shown me pictures of his family, and for the most part, I would "see" their faces, as he talked of them, so when I met some of them, I already knew who they were. We just flowed. They were amazed! I was so glad to see and meet all of the loved ones from his family stories!

"I feel like I've been knowing her forever!" somebody exclaimed.

"She don't seem like she's just meeting us for the first time!" said another.

"Well, Liston's talked of you all so much, I do feel like I already know you!"

They had such a beautiful cake specially made. His sister, Niecie, gifted me with a beautiful silver bracelet, and

Sacred Secret Seed

there were other gifts as well! They made me feel so special, so welcomed and so loved, and I still feel that way today.

I would meet and share a special bond with his sister, Ann, and her husband, Curtis, several months later.

His mother, Palm, is so sweet and funny. I had become accustomed to often sharing desserts with Liston, and I would feed us both. We were sitting at the table eating my birthday cake, and without even thinking, I would take a bite and then, feed him a bite.

Suddenly, Palm said, "Y'all see that?"

I looked around to see what she was talking about.

"Y'all see her feeding Liston like he's a baby or something?"

Some of them started giggling, while others just smiled. Liston and I chuckled, and I kept feeding him.

"Liston, what's wrong with your hands? You forgot how to use your own hands to eat? Umm-mm! Cliff! Where's Cliff?"

She was happy for us, but she was watching hard and didn't miss a beat!

I had informally met his mother one evening through Skype. Liston was at her house on his laptop talking with me, and she walked either in the room or by the room, and he called her to the computer to meet me, since she was being ... um....observant. She really just wanted a good look at me and didn't want herself to be in the camera, but Liston got her in there anyway to meet me. I knew then that I would have a ball with her! She already had me laughing inside.

His dad, Cliff Little, and I would talk for hours about Eastwood, its history, the people, stories, everything! Oh, did we enjoy reminiscing about our beloved Eastwood and our community of families! Anytime we started talking about Eastwood, we would be in a place of our own.

He also told funny stories about Liston as a kid, as well as stories about everybody and everything else. Every story Cliff told was either funny or quite interesting, especially stories about the "Professor."

Liston had already told me so many stories about "Mama and Daddy," Mrs. Julia and Mr. Richard Cherry, his grandparents. He had been born in their house on the coast of NC and had lived there with them for, at least, the first year of his life. When Mr. and Mrs. Cherry followed Palm and the rest of their children to New Jersey, Liston lived in his grandparents' NJ home as much as or more than he lived in his own. He even called them "Mama" and "Daddy." Liston grew up with all the privileges and benefits of being the only grandson, and he knew it.

Well, Cliff had a lot of stories of his own about "Mama" and "Professor" and especially about "Professor." Cliff and his father-in-law had worked together for many years, so he had a lot of stories to tell!

Cliff also gave everybody his own nicknames. He started calling me "Stuff" from the very beginning—hmm! Another Twilight Zone connection lies with Cliff's nicknames. His name for Liston is "Runt." Well, for several years before Liston found me, after he found me, and until I started eating healthy again, my *favorite* "go to" candy was Runts! I loved eating Runts, and when I traveled, I made sure to have two or three boxes of Runts in the car with me. In fact, earlier in our marriage, Liston kept me supplied with two or three boxes of Runts per purchase. He never just bought one box, unless there was only one box on the shelf. There have been so many uncanny connections revealed, since we have been together!

Being with Liston's entire family was and still is filled with love and fun. We all fell in love with each other, and that is the way life should be.

Two sunrises later ushered in Monday, December 17, 2012, my 50th birthday. Guess what? Did you guess? After so many years of wishing me, "Happy Birthday" where I could not hear him and three years of sending me birthday greetings through Facebook Messenger or inbox, My Baby finally—finally was able to audibly, from his lips to my ears, *and* face to face, wish—not just "Arlene Kearns"—but his fiancée,

"HAPPY BIRTHDAY, ARLENE KEARNS!!"

Whew! Had there been no other gifts, that alone would have been good enough for me! I don't think words can adequately explain the overwhelming joy and surreality of the moment when he spoke those historic words. He still showered me with love, flowers, balloons, fruit and a Kindle with a purple cover, my favorite color! I loved and appreciated all the gifts, but my special gift was priceless; it could not have been bought with money.

Now, it's time for our next adventure. Our excitement and nervousness continue, as we make final arrangements for both our Christmas night, intimate wedding ceremony as well as our trip to North Carolina for my 50th birthday dinner celebration and the introduction of Liston to my family!

We drove from Newport News to Pinehurst, Saturday morning, December 22. I had tried to arrange for my goddaughters to meet at my mother's house, so they could meet Liston before the big event later that evening, but our schedules were not working out. Liston and I were arriving later than planned.

When we arrived at my mother's, of course, there were a lot of introductions, hugs, questions, exclamations, smiles and laughter. Mother and Linda were extremely happy to finally meet Liston. After all, by this time, three months had passed since I told them I was engaged. They had been anticipating this moment for too long! We, finally, settled down and were just sitting around, casually, as they purposed to know all they could learn about my fiancé.

One of the first comments Mother made was, "Arlene, he looks just like your daddy. I can't believe how much he looks like your daddy!"

At one point, my mother and Liston were both sitting at the table. My mother stated bluntly, "You didn't ask me if you could marry my daughter."

What?? Ma!! I was shocked because that was nowhere in my mind at my age, but I didn't want to say anything, since she wasn't talking to me. I wanted to see how Liston was going to handle Test #1.

All eyes were on Liston, but the moment was a little comical for both of us, I think.

After his shock wore off, he said with a huge grin, "You're right. You're right, and I apologize. Mom, may I please have your daughter's hand in marriage?"

Liston has always called her Mom even from the beginning, and she has always called him, "Son."

She had this sneaky look about her and said, "Well, you're already engaged now, so I think you're pretty late with that, aren't you?"

Mama was working this one! I was chuckling softly and watching Liston's reactions. Liston was a trooper! He was saying and doing all the right things. Finally, Mother let him off the hook.

"She's certainly old enough, now, that I guess you wouldn't really need to ask me, but it would have been nice to have been considered. I am her mother."

"You're right, and I apologize, but look at her. You know your daughter. I love her so much. I couldn't let her get away from me, again!"

Mom laughed at that, and everything was okay.

Sacred Secret Seed

December 23, 2012

We had so many things to do and people to see before my dinner that we arrived there late. My goddaughters had already started calling and texting me to find out where we were. Oh no!

I thought we were "supposed" to arrive a little late, but my goddaughter, Allison, met us at the door assuring me, "No. You were supposed to arrive at 4:00, like I told you." She said the guests had arrived early, so they would all be there when I got there. "You're here now, so good. Come on!" She was serious but laughing, too, and I was trying to figure out why she was laughing. She was the first goddaughter to meet Liston, but it was quick, because she was hurrying us in.

She was right. Everybody was there already. They all clapped as we walked in. We were ushered all the way across the room to our special table, beautifully decorated and laid out for two, at the head and in the middle of everyone, so that all eyes could be on us. I guess they sang, but I don't remember because as I passed one after another, I was humored by the fact that their eyes were on Liston more than on me. Yes, I expected that, but can you at least speak to and celebrate me *first*?

That was one evening I could have used psychic powers! Oh, to hear the thoughts and whispers of everyone in that room!

I was so happy to see everyone who had come that evening to celebrate my 50th birthday and to meet my fiancé! My cousin, Betanya, had come in from Charlotte, and my friend, Jamala, and her mother had come all the way from Maryland! Several other friends and relatives were there, and my goddaughters had just outdone themselves!

After the introduction and a prayer, the line for the food began, and so did social hour. Since my daughters were bringing Liston and me our plates, we started to walk around and greet everyone, personally, thanking them for coming and introducing them to Liston. However, so many were coming to us, first, to speak and to welcome Liston. After greeting the loving and so appreciated welcoming party, we began our tour around the tables.

Most of my family greeted and welcomed Liston warmly, but there were a couple of extended family members who gave him the cold, metal face. I mean, who was this dude who proposed to Arlene without even meeting his family? Her father is no longer with us, but she does have a mother, still. What's on his mind? Is he going to treat her right? She's waited all these years. Who is this man that she kept secret, and why?

We understood. I had already prepared him. They actually were not as tough as I thought they would be. After Liston passed the initial shake down unmoved, I guess they figured he was all right. My first cousin, Tessie, gave him a warm, Kearns welcome hug.

"We hug in this family, and you're part of us, now. I can tell you're making Arlene happy, and that's what matters. I just wish her father were here to see this day! I'm just so happy for the both of you, and as the oldest granddaughter of the family, I welcome you to our Kearns family, and I love you because you love her! How about that?"

Liston gave her one of his tight bear hugs.

"Whew! Okay. That was a real hug!" and with that, she went on her way.

He met my sisters who had not been at my mother's earlier that day: Wanda, Beverly and Brenda; my oldest brother, Franklin, and he remembered Danny from that summer at the community center; my other brothers: Dwight and Teddy; my Uncle Halbert, who is my father's youngest brother and the patriarch of the Kearns family; another first cousin, Jackie, whose main purpose that night was to see all the way through this man who had, somehow, stolen her cousin's heart. She intended to make sure he understood her facial and body language, "You better treat her right. You better never hurt her. You mess up one time, Fella, just one …" Jackie—was not playing! Shoot! She barely even looked at me for staring him down, and "I" was scared! My uncle was doing the same that night through looks, body language and words, but the next time Uncle Halbert saw Liston, I think he loved him as much as everyone else did because he could see my joy and happiness.

He met some of my godchildren: Allison, Kimberly, Lavonia, Benita, Moncello and Angel; my god sister who is more like my daughter, Ebony; my niece-daughter, Amber; my nephew, Rinardo and his sons: Zeldon and Sabien; Little Sabien's head didn't even reach the edge of our table, but without asking and quick as lightning, he reached his little thick arm up to Liston's slice of birthday cake, wiped his finger through the icing, and carried it to his mouth; Rinardo's wife, Tyniece, had spoken to and partially introduced herself to Liston in the store earlier that day, recognizing him from Facebook pictures; my cousin, Betanya, and so many more! He had already met Jamala at the National Book Festival on the National Mall in DC in September, the week right after we were engaged. She is also the one who saw his original inbox message after I read it and heard my screams the night of June 29, 2009.

Out of all my family and friends whom Liston met that night, only one seriously concerned him. This was a man with facial hair who wore an old woman's grey wig, wore an old woman's dress, and carried an old woman's pocketbook on his arm, but walked around manly, and everybody treated him as if it was normal. I had hugged him, glad to see him and introduced him to Liston, yet Liston received no explanation. Liston was reluctant to ask me about this relative who had obvious problems, since no one seemed to be concerned, but Liston was bothered. Here was a young man who, for some reason, wanted to be—not just a woman—but an old woman! Well, he didn't seem to want to be a woman, because he didn't try to change his character. He walked like a man, talked like a man, acted like a man, but dressed like an old woman! He didn't even shave or keep a close cut to try to look like a woman! To Liston, this guy had serious issues! "Why aren't they concerned?!" he wondered. "Why are they acting like this is normal?"

Well, the program was starting! My daughters had planned so well! Ebony was the Mistress of Ceremony; Ms. Dickerson mimed, and so many family members and loved ones had remarks that just warmed my heart!

When they called for "Aunt Ida," the man in the dress stood.

"They even call her by a woman's name! What is going on here?" Liston thought in total confusion.

Aunt Ida began to do her routine, as she roasted me. She was hilarious and had everyone rolling! It took Liston a couple of minutes, but he finally understood with laughter and much relief that the young man did not just walk around town wearing old women's clothing. That was my nephew, Terry, and he was wearing his costume for his comedy role, "Aunt Ida."

Boy was Liston relieved! What a night!

My goddaughters really created a fun, loving and wonderful night to celebrate my 50th birthday! I love them so much!

Chapter 16
Mother & Aunt Mae

My mother used the next two days to try to get to know Liston as much as possible. They had conversations, sometimes, as if I was not even present. They sat together at the table. They sat together on the love couch. I found out, later, they had their deepest conversations when I was not around them.

Sometimes, Mother was funny. She mostly seemed happy, but other moments, she was solemn and pensive. Sometimes, she was serious, but all the time, she was loving and sweet. I guess her mind was on all that a mother would think about when her youngest daughter is getting married. I think, too, that she was thinking of Daddy who had transitioned seven Decembers earlier, wishing he was present to witness all of this. I am the only daughter he was not able to see married.

Liston told me, later, that Mother asked him, "Please, please take care of that one. You have a special one right there, and she's waited a long time for this. I wish you had come a long time ago, but now that you're here, I need you to take care of her for me. She's dear to me. Will you promise me that you'll take care of her?"

He assured her, "You don't have to worry about that, Mom. I've waited more than 34 years for Arlene. I've loved her for a very long time. Now, that I've found her, I'm not about to let anything happen to her. I've made it my life's mission to take care of her and to make sure she's happy."

The next day was Christmas Eve. I was supposed to be ready by a certain time that morning, because Liston was coming to get me. Of course, I was dragging around, so I wasn't quite ready when he arrived. Linda had kept telling me I needed to hurry up and get ready because I knew Liston was coming. I could hear Mother and Linda ragging on me, but I couldn't hear Liston's responses. Of course, I simply ignored their comments, while chuckling within myself. They knew they were happy for me, regardless of my shortcomings or late comings.

When I was ready and walking toward the dining room where they were all sitting, I could hear my mother calmly praising him, "You must be a patient man."

Then, Linda chimes in, of course. "Hey! You sho' must be! You gotta be with Arlene! Shoot!"

I'm fully in the same room with them now, so I ask jovially as I go to greet Liston, "He's gotta be what with me?"

Linda snorts, "Humph!"

She's so funny!

I would always try to visit Aunt Mae when I was in town, and I definitely wanted her to meet Liston, so we went to see her first. As always, seeing Aunt Mae and spending time with her was such a joy! She was giddy and so surprised but happy when I told her I was getting married. She used to love saying that somebody "got a boyfriend!"

When I told her we were getting married, she did a double-take. Then, she just stared at me as if to make sure I was serious and not joking around, or maybe to make sure she had heard me correctly. Then, this huge smile crawled across her face, and she covered her mouth, as she began to laugh.

"Married? You and him?" She pointed with her fingers.

I was sitting on the bed beside her, and Liston was sitting in a chair across from her.

"Yep!" I confirmed, and I showed her my ring on my finger.

She softly grabbed my hand, and while she was looking at my ring, she sounded, "Mmm." She repeatedly lifted her head to look right in my eyes questioning, like she couldn't believe it.

She looked at both of us again. She asked to reconfirm, "You and him gettin' married?"

"Yes, Mae! We're getting married!" Liston and I both had these huge, crazy smiles across our faces.

Then, she laughed shyly and said, "Okay den."

We spent the next minutes to an hour singing Christmas carols and chatting, while Liston recorded us and took pictures. I love my Aunt Mary! She's my sweetheart!

Christmas Eve 2012

Back at my mother's, the time had come to reveal to her that we would not be staying for the "Kearns Family Annual Christmas Celebration."

She was so disappointed, as I knew she would be. "What? You're not gonna be here for Christmas? Huh? Why?"

Oh, I hated not being totally forthcoming with my Mother about our plans! How I wish I could have just zipped her away with us, so she could be there at my wedding with me! I knew that would be a problem, and I did not want to make her choose whether to leave the family at Christmas to be with me or to let me get married without her and stay there with the family. I was not going to make her choose for her to be sad about whichever choice she made. Although if she had gone with me, she would not have had much time to be sad!

The reason Liston and I agreed to have the ceremony privately is because Christmas is a big, special time for both our families. Both homes of our parents were and are the hub of Christmas Day: family and friends, events, feasting and gifting. Our dinners are family annual events. I knew that our families would try to talk us out of getting married on Christmas night, and that would cause problems. Some of them would have come, but my family members who did not come could possibly be upset with the ones who did. Then, they could have an issue with me as well because I caused the division at Christmas. So, I thought this was the best way—to just keep everything a secret until after our public wedding in April. I wanted to give everyone the opportunity to feel the excitement and awe of watching me finally get married!

I explained to Mother, "A friend is getting married Christmas night in Maryland, and I really need to be there." *That was true.*

"Christmas? Well! Are you in the wedding?"

"Yes. That's why I have to be there. I can't let them down." *That also was true.*

"Well, okay. I understand that, but I sure do hate you're not gonna be here for Christmas!"

"Well, I will be here tomorrow morning, but I just have to leave early." I think we had to leave by 9:00 or 10:00, so we might have had breakfast with her before we left.

That Christmas Eve, the three of us were able to share quite a bit. Later, she called me down to her room, and we talked even more. Our talks and time spent together that day were so meaningful to me, because I knew I was getting married the next night without her presence. God knew this, and He was aligning everything perfectly! You would have thought she knew! She didn't though. She had no idea. She just knew I would be married in April, so she wanted to share her heart. She even shared my father's heart—what she thought he would want to say to me. Words they had shared concerning me before he left the earth. The discussion in my mother's room that day was so special and meaningful and definitely God-ordained. She even gave me a special gift. She did not know that I would be getting married the next night, but my Father—God knew.

Chapter 17
Harvest Time!

It's my WEDDING DAY!!!! Oh, my God! This is really happening! Plans are enacted! People are in place! We stop at my house in Newport News on the way to Gaylord National which is just outside of Washington, DC. We have to gather all the clothing, accessories and items we need, but before we left for NC, we packed and placed everything for quick pick-up:

- ✓ Wedding arch
- ✓ Flowers
- ✓ Lights
- ✓ Candles and holder
- ✓ Runner
- ✓ Mini communion set
- ✓ Items for rope ceremony
- ✓ Music

- ✓ Marriage license
- ✓ Bouquet and boutonnière
- ✓ Kneeling bench/pillows
- ✓ Rings
- ✓ Everything else!

As we travel toward our destination, the excitement level and emotions are well over the top, and I simply cannot control them! I am so thankful that I created lists before, so that I would not have to "think," because, right now, I am in straight "feel" mode, excited that this day has finally come! I am really getting married, after all these years!! I am getting married to LISTON! What?? How unbelievable is THAT?!

> *My family is not going to be there. My mother is not here with me. They don't even know! Am I really doing this without my mother? HOW am I doing this without her?? Oh, God! This is unbelievable! How did all of this come together so perfectly? Father, give me strength, and help me not to fall apart.*
>
> *Oh, no! I forgot something special to wear for him tonight! I planned it in my mind, but I forgot to purchase it! How did I forget something so important? My mind reminisces to the clothing items I did bring. Okay. I have something. I have to make it work. He's not going to care. He'll be looking past it anyway.*

So, it's probably not as important to him as it is to me. It's not what I had in my mind, but this will have to do. Maybe one of the hotel shops will still be open, and I can purchase something ... or maybe not; this is Christmas Day. Hmm? I'll keep my eyes open after we check in and get everything ready. We'll have to walk around on our way to dinner.

When Liston returns to the suite with the bellman, bringing the last items, I am already well into decorating the room. I want everything complete and ready early to reduce anxiety, nervousness, frantic rushing and frustration. I want the day to be wonderful, peaceful and happy all day! It is MY WEDDING DAY!! Wow!

After the bellman leaves, Liston is just standing there silently, looking strange and worried.

"Are you okay?" I ask.

He doesn't say anything, yet. He looks like he's trying to figure something out.

I'm still busily decorating, but I'm watching him, too. "What's wrong?"

He finally says, "I—I need to talk to you about something."

He looks so defeated, like he's about to burst into tears on our wedding day! I stop working, and now, I'm the one staring. What could he possibly need to talk to me about?

He looks right into my eyes.

"I'm sorry, Sweetness."

"What?" I'm wondering what on earth could have gone wrong that quickly! Did something happen to the car? What?

"I know you want our wedding to be perfect, and you've worked so hard to make sure everything was in place …"

He pauses, and I'm silently listening, waiting for him to finish.

"I think I left my shoes at the hotel in North Carolina. I'm sorry, Baby. I was doing my best to make sure I had them and that nothing happened to them. I put them in the top of the closet in the room because I didn't want them to get mixed up with the gifts in the car and get left behind somehow. I—I forgot they were up there, I guess. I was hoping I was wrong, and that I had actually put them in the car, but I don't have them. I'm sorry, Sweetness. I was really trying to make sure everything was perfect for you."

"Oh. Okay." I smile to try to put him at ease, and because I am relieved that it's not a serious problem after all. "What shoes do you have?"

"Just these that I'm wearing."

I look down, and although they are not polished, dress shoes, they are nice, black and look fine to me.

"What's wrong with those?"

"Well, nothing is wrong with them, but I don't wear these with a suit. They're not my dress shoes, but-- these are okay?"

"Of course, Baby. They're okay. How long have you been worried about that without saying something?"

Whew! What a relief! Is he kidding? I am not about to let anything that minor become a problem! He can have white sneakers for all I care today!

Soon, we decide to go ahead and get dinner. As we walk through the resort, I scan the shops to see what is open. The only shops that are still open are those related to coffee, snacks or small souvenirs, so the apparel I did bring will have to do. I decide that the importance, more than the apparel itself, will be the way I work it. Um-hm.

On the way back to the suite, I am calmer and more at peace. I guess I got all the jitters out earlier. I am more comfortable, now, with all the major work already complete.

My friend and sister, Karen Joseph, from my church, Greater Mt. Calvary in DC will be singing for the ceremony. She arrives early to make sure I have everything I need, to help decorate and to help however she can. Shortly afterwards, my friend from childhood, Karen Alston, professional photographer and graphics designer, arrives with her sons. She wants to capture the moments before and after the wedding as well, so professional! Yes! One son will operate the music for me; another one will record the wedding on video for me, while she does all the still photography!

As Karen J fills in so perfectly for my sisters, maid of honor, make-up artist *and* wedding director, Karen A is capturing all the moments! Karen A floats from my room to wherever Liston is waiting, to the ceremony area, everywhere—creating just the right photos with various wedding decorations and objects!

Karen J applies my make-up, helps me get dressed, continues to make sure everything is operating fluently and properly outside my room and also checks on Liston to make sure he has everything he needs.

One of my former colleagues, Shelton Sullivan, became a great brother to me. He is also a minister and either an Associate or an Assistant Pastor for his church. He was more than happy to be the officiant over our ceremony and marry Liston and me. He and his wife arrive well within their schedule. She will be one of the witnesses to sign our marriage certificate.

There is so much energy, hustle and bustle in this suite tonight! My room door opens just enough for one of the Karens to get through. I glance through the opening and see my groom sitting comfortably in a chair not far from my room door. He is already dressed and just waiting for the ceremony to begin. Oh, I love him so much! The wedding is scheduled for 10:00 P.M. Everyone is in place. I am all ready. IT'S TIME!

Karen J, caught up in the atmosphere, decides the bride cannot go up the aisle without flowers strewn first, so now, she has yet another role! She is, proudly, my flower girl, and what a beautiful flower girl she makes! I am glad she thought of that!

Now, it is my turn. It is my time to walk up the aisle to my groom! I don't need anyone to give me away, legally. Come on, I am fifty years old! I walk that walk with God, alone, happy, excited, pensive, and in love. I walk out of the room and onto my path— and stand.

I am staring at my handsome groom, and he is staring back at his gorgeous bride. The music begins, and so do I. I open my mouth and begin to sing a song about my groom.

> *At ... last, my love has come along.*
> *My lonely days are over,*
> *and life is like a song.*
> *Oh yeah ... yeah.*

He's standing at attention with that special smile on his face, meant just for me.

> *At last, the skies above are blue.*
> *My heart was wrapped up in clover*
> *the [day] I looked at you.*
> *I found a dream that I could speak to,*
> *a dream that I can call my own.*
> *I found a thrill to press my cheek to,*

Dr. Arlene Kearns Dowdy

a thrill that I have never known,
Oh, oh, oh

Look at him! He is so thrilled! I love that man so much!

You smiled, you smiled,

Sacred Secret Seed

and then, the spell was cast.
And here we are in Heaven.
For you are mine at last.
[Songwriter, Mack Gordon- 1941;
as sung by Etta James, 1959]

There is unexpected clapping and hushed exclamations of "Wow!" I almost forgot about the others! I was so focused on My Baby! Even Liston claps. Look at him! I know he wants to just sweep me up right now!

I walk up the aisle to my groom, as the music ends. He hasn't taken his eyes off me even once, and I haven't taken mine off him, either.

Just as I get to the altar for the ceremony and break our glance to face the preacher, the feeling hits me again that my mother is not here.

"How can I be doing this without my mother?
Do I really want to do this without her? I don't
have to do this, now! I can wait!"

I turn and look again at Liston, and all those doubtful, anxious, lonely thoughts just fade away. I only need him to be here. Peace comes over me again, and I am at rest, at rest in love.

Dr. Arlene Kearns Dowdy

My Baby polished and SHINED those shoes!

Shelton is working this wedding ceremony! He is even smoothly working into his ritual, the extra rope ceremony that I added. Wow! Where did he get his ceremony from? These words are so meaningful! Yep! God led me to ask the right one! No wonder, though. I've always known Shelton S to be honest, humble, gentle and kind.

Look at My Baby! This is so perfect! He is so perfect! Thank You, Jesus! I am getting married! This is my wedding! This is really happening! It won't be much longer now!

Karen A's camera is everywhere! She is trying her best to capture every moment! I love it! I love the way she works! Oh, that looks like a great shot! I can't wait to see these pictures!

Is this it? Yes! The ceremony is over! Here it comes!

"I, now, pronounce you Man and Wife."

We did it! GOD did it! We are married! We are finally married!

Dr. Arlene Kearns Dowdy

Karen J starts singing, as we stand facing the few in the audience. She sings Liston's song to his bride:

> *"For once in my life, I have someone who needs me, someone I've needed so long. For once, unafraid, I can go where life leads me, and somehow I know I'll be strong. For once I can touch what my heart used to dream of, long before I knew, someone warm like you would make my dreams come true…"*
> [Stevie Wonder, December 8, 1968]

Although I was uncertain and apologetic when I asked people to leave their families and homes on Christmas night to be a part of our wedding, every single person we asked to be a part was overjoyed, excited and even felt honored to be asked to bless our union. I know that God led me to them. We were and are so grateful to them—so grateful! They blessed and were a part of one of the absolutely best days of my life!

Karen A took many pictures there in the suite, down the hall, to the elevator, and all around the resort, working in its Christmas beauty!

Oh, what a glorious night!! So very glorious!

I've always loved snow, and I've always loved the beauty of Christmas decorations. The combination of snow at Christmas, to me, is one of the most beautiful sights in the world! The seven years I lived in Alaska gave me that beautiful gift every year!

The morning after our Christmas wedding welcomed us with snow. We stood there at that big, picture window in each other's arms as husband and wife, Mr. and Mrs. Clay Liston Dowdy. We watched as our Heavenly Father blessed us, now, with this beautiful and peaceful sight—a blanket of snow on the ground, snow falling silently and gracefully from the sky and reflections of colorful Christmas lights all around us. How could life get any better than this?!

Since we didn't need the suite anymore after our wedding, we were blessed to have yet another friend and former colleague, Alejandria, who wanted to bless us with our room for the next few days and nights. She took time out of her schedule to meet us at the resort the next day to ensure smooth arrangements. We so appreciated her loving care! She was probably there just five minutes with a big smile on her face and was the only friend to see us on our honeymoon.

Our days there were filled with bliss, love, joy, Christmas beauty and snow! We are married! We are Mr. and Mrs. Clay Liston Dowdy!

Now, seven years later, I research the name "Karen" for any significance to the fact that the only two female friends participating in our wedding bore that name. The first definition I read tells me the name is of Danish origin meaning "pure" (nameberry.com). I believe everything God does is significant. Maybe we were both being purified in order to start our marriage totally pure. Hmm.

Chapter 18
On Display

In January, I returned to my job at Hampton High School as Dr. D or Dr. Dowdy—no more Dr. K or Dr. Kearns. The students and other teachers had tried to prepare themselves in December before our winter break. I had practiced singing my song in front of them. They had watched our video stories and fell in love with our relationship. They were excited, and they all knew about our upcoming public wedding and wanted to attend. I told them they were all invited, but I knew the likelihood of any of them being able to travel to NC was minimal. I would share the pictures and videos upon my return.

Fortunately, for my students, I had chosen not to leave them and my position as Reading Specialist in the middle of the academic year. I would wait and leave after graduation.

Dr. Arlene Kearns Dowdy

All the plans for my public wedding were being made and arranged from Virginia with no close relatives near me. Meanwhile, Liston was in search of the just-right house in the just-right place to bring his wife—the place we would call "home." We were in high anticipation for when we would be living under one roof as husband and wife.

Although I did not have immediate family near me, a family friend and sister, Lorraine, also lived in Newport News. Lorraine probably knows almost every member of my family and extended families, and I know her family. She and her sister, Althea, spent days and nights in my parents' house, as I did in theirs. We would talk for hours upon hours.

She came through for me to help in different ways, like being with me on that very important occasion when I picked out my wedding gown. I don't know why I didn't think about going to Eastwood to bring my mother back with me for a week when I scheduled my appointment. I was so independent that I was just going through the steps, I guess. I didn't even plan Lorraine's presence with me. She just happened to call either that same day or the evening before.

"What you got going on this week?" she asked me.

"Well, for one, I have an appointment at David's Bridal to pick out my gown."

"Ohhh! Who's going with you?"

"Um, I hadn't thought about anybody going with me. I guess I'm going alone. Do I need somebody with me?"

"Lene, you don't go pick out a wedding dress by yourself! Let me see if I can make some arrangements to meet you there."

"Okay. That'll be good, Rayne, if you can get there. Thanks. I just hadn't thought about someone being there with me."

There I was missing out on yet another mother-daughter event, I guess. My mind was so filled with Liston!

Lorraine also came over to help with crafts or bagging souvenirs. She was funny trying to figure out steps and making everything come together. She would give up on one part and ask, "You got sum'n else I can do. I just can't get that!" It was nice having family from home helping me or just to have someone there to share while I worked.

I know that other friends, family members and godchildren would have jumped in a car and spent weekends there to help me if I had asked them. I just didn't think about it.

One of my sisters, Wanda, did tell me to take my wedding programs home with me, and she would help fold them. There was a special fold for those programs, so I was glad to receive their help. Several of us, including Beverly, Wanda and my mother, gathered around the table and folded our programs until they were complete!

Also during this time, my matron of honor, my niece-daughter Sharonda, was busy at work planning my bridal shower! It was held in the home of my mother and was a lingerie party! Boy, did we laugh and cut up at that shower! In the midst of the laughter and tears (from laughing so hard), I heard somebody say, "I don't think I've ever had this much fun at a bridal shower!" We had crazy fun!

Liston's sister, Ann, was devastated that she would not be able to make it to the wedding because of her job, but she sent an early gift along with such a sweet note that made me anxious to meet her. Also, my mother's eldest aunt, Aunt Lucille, sent an early gift and a note that because of her health, she would not be able to attend. Both of these notes remain dear to me to this day.

As the big day of April 6, 2013 drew closer, Wanda and one of my first cousins, Cliff "Bab", wanted to take care of the flowers for my wedding! Bab had been more like an older brother through the years, especially after my father passed away. I thought that was so sweet of them. I let them know they didn't have to do anything, but they really wanted to help in some way. They were a blessing! My bouquet, created and arranged by Ruth Hazel McRae, was so beautiful! Another long-time friend and sister, Wanda Gillespie, wife of Deacon Felton Gillespie and Ruth Hazel's baby sister, made my wedding cakes. Lord, that was more like a "system" or a "display of cakes"! Not only was the display just gorgeous, but the cake was heavenly delicious! You know, she would not let me pay her for my wedding cakes!! Some people have such beautiful hearts that you just want to send them on a cruise or something, you know?

The day of the big wedding that I had prayed and waited decades to witness was fast approaching! My bridal house was ready; my maid of honor, Nancy Smith, arrived a couple of days early from Anchorage, Alaska, to spend time with me and help make sure everything was in order.

Since Nancy and I spent the first few hours at the bridal house alone that evening, I wanted to reveal the news of our first wedding to her. I gave her my mini camcorder and told her to press play.

"Ahhh! Oh, my God!" She knew exactly what was happening. "You're already married?!" Then, "Ohhh, you sang to him!"

Nancy cried as she watched me getting married to Liston. "I'm so happy for you! I can't believe this!"

~~*~~

Liston's buddies, also, were already arriving at the hotel designated for the groomsmen; the pivotal leaders had arrived at the hotel designated for them, including Pastor Sean all the way from the Middle Eastern country of Abu Dhabi, and our family and friends from everywhere were arriving and checking in to their accommodations. Even while we were at the church for the wedding rehearsal, in walk my friends all the way from Nigeria, Africa! To this day, I have not been able to express to them just how much their coming and presence meant to me! My sister Tracy accepted to be one of my bridesmaids, even though it would mean long, tedious travel. Her husband, Olalekan, and friend, Obioma, both special brothers of mine, also traveled the distance! What pure love was shown to us by everyone!

During the rehearsal is also when Liston showed his best man, Steve, pictures from our first wedding, surprising him with the news that we were already married.

There was much ado around Moore County! Love, excitement and expectancy were heavily in the air!

To tell you everything about that day would probably be another book entirely! Aside from a few technology glitches that caused delays for the reception, the wedding and reception were just exceptional! I am so glad we have photographs and videos that tell the story!

When we looked back at the video later, I saw people that I did not even know were present! One after another would bring an exclamation, "Oh! ____ was there?! Oh, wow!" "____ was there, too?!" My husband has always said, "That day was such a blur! I can't tell you much of anything that happened, let alone tell you who was there!"

My Uncle Halbert, my father's youngest brother and look-alike, consented to walk me down the aisle to give me away. I love that man so much!

We are so very grateful for every individual who thought of Liston and me so much that you came from near and far to be with us for our special wedding day. We appreciate each individual and company who helped in every way to make that entire weekend of April 6, 2013 so extravagant and memorable! You are the best, and we love you all! (A copy of the wedding program and party is included at the back of this book.)

Dr. Arlene Kearns Dowdy

Chapter 19
Aruba!

That night, we departed from the reception in my wedding gift from my husband. Liston had a Saab 93 that was his "baby." He loves that car! However, he informed me that he wanted me to accept it as my own car, a wedding gift from him. He was giving his former "baby" to his new "Sweetness". Wow! I had never owned a convertible! Aside from my father, no one had ever gifted me with a car! What love! What a man! What a nice car!

I have a convertible! Although I didn't name her at first, later, I named her "Mae Lane" after my precious aunt, Mary Lane.

After our departure from the reception, we began our journey to the place of our honeymoon. My husband had chosen to take me to the beautiful, gorgeous island of

Aruba! We spent several days in Oranjestad, the capital city of the island.

Aruba's waters are so gorgeous; the beaches and resorts are top-notch, and we were married! We were man and wife, and now, everyone knew!

Aruba is an island north of Venezuela known for its absolutely amazing beaches, with water so clear we could see right through to the bottom! I have seen the waters of the Bahamas as well as Jamaica, and their waters are beautiful, too, but there was still a special difference about the waters of Aruba with its white sand beaches. Maybe the difference was that this was my honeymoon, and I was with my husband!

Flamingos, sand crabs and large iguanas were abundant! If you were going to walk across a field, you had to be careful and watch where you were going, because the field could be strewn with iguanas sunning! They did not seem to be dangerous though. Nobody seemed to mind them, and they did not seem to mind people. We were all at peace with one another!

The weather was perfect! The sun was not glaring; the breeze from the wind was glorious, and there was no humidity! Aruba is actually known for having consistently fine weather. We absolutely love Aruba, and we absolutely love each other, so we had a lovely time being in love in Aruba!

Sacred Secret Seed

Something else special happened while we were there in Aruba. Liston was baptized! During one of our discussions there, Liston mentioned that he had never been baptized.

I don't remember if we had discussed this before, but since we were discussing it, I asked him, "Would you like to get baptized now, while we're on our honeymoon, right here in Aruba?"

"I can do that?" he asked.

"Yes!"

"Well, what would I need to do? What do we do to make that happen here?" He was excitedly curious and interested in knowing how he could finally be baptized!

"As an ordained and licensed elder, I can baptize you. I would be honored to baptize my husband." I had performed baptisms before, and to baptize my own husband would be a special joy.

We discussed the process of baptism and studied the spiritual and biblical importance, the meaning and the obedience of being baptized. We did all the preliminaries before going down to the water, so that when we got there, all we needed to do was the brief baptism itself: a short song, a prayer, the submerging, more song and words from Liston. That moment was yet another serene and divine experience. If anyone paid attention to us, I wasn't aware. My attention was only on the three of us: The Holy Spirit, Liston and myself.

When it was time to depart Aruba, we met a couple who said they made the trip from New Jersey at least once per month! We looked at each other and declared that we definitely wanted to go back to Aruba often.

Chapter 20
The Reveal

Upon our return to Eastwood, the time of revealing had come. Now, they would learn about our first wedding and our actual marriage date. I had contemplated how I would do this. Of course, my mother would be told first.

I took my mini camcorder into the dining and sitting room where my mother spends most of her time at home.

"Here, Mom. I want you to see something."

"What is it?" she asks excitedly.

I placed the camera on the table in front of her with the small screen toward her. "I want you to watch this."

As she watched the screen, I watched her, having no idea whatsoever how she would react to the news.

"Huh?! What is this? Arlene? Come on!"

I put the video on pause and told her everything. She seemed to have a mixture of confusion, surprise, humor and ... gratitude, for some reason, and she understood. I even reminded her of the meaningful sharing and conversation the two of us had that Christmas Eve night and how God had aligned that so intentionally.

"Well, let me see. I wanna watch the rest of it!" she announces. She holds the camera closer to her.

I click play and wait while she watches the rest of the wedding, answering her questions throughout.

"That's you? You sang to him?!" She was loving it!

"Yes, ma'am!"

"Who's the preacher that's marrying you?"

"A friend, someone I used to work with. He's a minister at a church in Maryland or DC."

"Wow! I like him! ... He's good!"

"Mmm-hmm!"

Sometime after she finishes watching our wedding, she said, "So all that worrying and praying I was doing for you when y'all went on that honeymoon, I didn't have to be doing."

I couldn't do anything but laugh, "Aww ... I'm sorry you worried, but we still needed your prayers. We always need your prayers!" She was so funny, but I was glad she was pleased and satisfied.

Liston told me that in, yet, another conversation, Mother shocked him by stating, "I guess you aren't as patient as I thought you were."

My mother is hilarious and full of shockers! Apparently, her earlier statement had nothing to do with his waiting on me, when I was late getting ready that December morning!

When Liston returned to NJ, he revealed the news to his mother. Since he didn't have the video, he showed her pictures from our first wedding. At first, she didn't figure it out.

"What am I looking at?" she asked him.

"You don't notice anything?" Liston asked.

Then, he also showed her some pictures from the second wedding—the one she had attended.

Suddenly, as she realized what she was seeing, she was even more confused, so Liston explained.

"Oh! Well, why did you have to have two weddings?" she asked after he explained.

A man of few words, Liston says slowly, "She's ....a minister."

Understanding now, Mom replies, "Oh. Oh! Okay, then. Good! Y'all did the right thing!"

We are both thankful and appreciative for parents who are wise and understanding.

Dr. Arlene Kearns Dowdy

Chapter 21
Going Home

After months of house searching, even before our second wedding, Liston finally found "the house" in "the neighborhood" for us. He knew that he had married a "country girl," who does not like driving in the city. Sure, I had traveled by land, air and sea. However, I still do not like city driving. I could and can drive in the city. I just do not like it. Driving in busy traffic in the city is stressful! So, he found a house in an area similar to where I had lived when I was in Newport News. He found a house in an area with nearby restaurants, businesses and shopping areas but also with fields, animals, markets and even farms!

"When can you get here to see it?" he wanted to know.

"I need to come there? I can already tell from the pictures and description that I like it," I tried to assure him.

"This house is for you. The pictures don't tell the whole story. I don't want to settle on a house that you haven't even seen."

"Okay. Should I come this weekend?"

"I was hoping you would say that! Let me check with the realtor and the inspectors to make sure everything can happen Saturday."

Liston arranged everything. I liked the house and the area a lot! While Liston and the realtor were giving me a tour, the inspectors started to arrive. One inspector, after another, spoke about how impressed he was with the house, letting Liston know that he had a nice one. While the inspectors conducted their searches, Liston and I sat at the kitchen table chatting with the realtor.

When the final inspector was finished, Liston and I had already been there for a few hours. We were hungry and ready to eat, and I was tired after my five-hour drive. Everyone shook hands. The men congratulated Liston. He and the realtor made some arrangements, and we left.

We found, right there in the community, a big market place with a Dutch market on one end, and we had a ball! The food, breads, desserts, meats, everything looked and smelled delicious! After we ate, we drove around for a while to get a look at the surroundings. Soon, I guess the both of us were tired.

"I guess it's time to turn in now," suggested Liston.

I agreed. "Yeh, I'm pretty tired after the drive."

After a few minutes, Liston said, "Oh! I was headed back to the house!"

Momentarily confused, I looked at him and asked, "Well, where *are* we going?"

He looked at me to give me a moment. When I was still waiting on his answer, Liston smiled and reminded me, "The house is not ours yet. We checked into a hotel this morning, remember?"

"Oh, yeh! Wow!"

Both of us had felt so comfortable and at home while sitting in that kitchen talking with the realtor, that the house already felt like "home." The fact that both of us forgot all about the hotel, and our minds were back at the house was simply amazing!

We closed on the house May 10, 2013! After that, we started meeting in our home and "camping out." We had appliances but no furniture yet because the furniture was in my house in Virginia and in storage. We used the beach chairs that were always in the trunk of my car to sit in when we weren't sitting on the floor and an air mattress for our bed. Each weekend, I would move some items, like linens, clothes and dishes or whatever I could get packed and in the car. We would use my Kindle or a laptop, if we wanted to watch TV or a movie. We really enjoyed those weekends camping out in our home with only the bare amenities!

Camping out with my husband in our own home was so romantic!

I had so much to pack in so little time! Since I would be working all the way up to moving day, Liston's family was planning to rent a van, so a lot of them could come to my house and help me pack up. They figured with all their help, I would be packed up in one weekend.

I was so floored when Liston told me that! They are a really sweet and thoughtful family. As much as I knew I needed and even wanted that to happen, I didn't want them to go to that expense. They also would have had to rent hotel rooms, because my house was too compact for all of them.

Around the end of May or first of June, my mother came to Newport News to help me pack. She knew the difficulty I was facing, trying to pack everything by June 14. I don't remember if I picked her up or if she rode up from NC with Lorraine. By the end of Mother's visit, although she had done so much, there was still a lot more that needed to be done. She kept saying, "If I just had two or three more days, I think I could finish this!" I don't remember what was happening in NC or why she could not stay, but she wasn't able to stay those two or three days past her scheduled time. She really wanted to complete what she came to do. She must not have realized just how much she accomplished while I was at work! I don't know what I would have done without her! I probably would have consented for Liston's family to rent that van and come on down in spite of the expense!

Educators know that the last week of school is a busy week for teachers! We have final grade reports; promotion or non-promotion reports; room clean-up; check lists to complete and get signed off; scholars submitting last-minute assignments, hoping they will be accepted, so they can graduate or pass; one teachers' meeting after another; parent calls and/or meetings; discipline and counseling continue; former student visits; award programs, and all sorts of end-of-year activities.

Well, I was doing all that *and* trying to finish my packing. It's amazing how much "stuff" can be hidden in a small, compact house!

During this time, My Baby was also busy. He was coming to get his wife to take her home! He was busy with all types of arrangements. He booked a one-way flight from Newark to Newport News. He booked a large U-Haul truck with all the accessories for a one-way trip, booked a moving company in Virginia to pack my belongings on the truck, and booked his friend's moving company in NJ to unpack the truck and move everything into our new home. My husband, too, was busy!

The last day of school and high school graduation was Friday, June 14, 2013. Liston arrived Thursday and picked up the moving truck. He helped with final packing and organized all the boxes that were already packed. Friday night, my husband accompanied me to the graduation, but we were able to leave the graduation early to continue packing.

The next day, the movers came to pack the truck. We were *still* packing! Occasionally, I would hear a sigh from my husband, and he would glance at me as if to say, "Where in the world did all this stuff come from? Do you really need all this?" He didn't say anything though. He just kept working. He just wanted to finish and get his wife home. If I had managed my time better or had more time to manage, I honestly would have had a garage sale before moving!

Sacred Secret Seed

Liston also had the movers to retrieve the boxes and items from the storage unit behind the house. I had already shown him which items in the storage unit were mine and the few items that were already in there when I moved into the house.

By the time the movers had finished with their professional packing, except for a few personal bags that would go with me in the car, all my packing was complete! But there was a problem. The movers brought back inside a couple of items they couldn't fit into the truck. My car was packed safely for the five-hour drive, and the items could not go in there, either.

We were all standing there looking at each other. I was in silent dismay. I did not know what to say or do. I finally suggested we leave them with my neighbor across the street and come through, later, to get them. My husband dismissed the company of movers, and I could tell that he was contemplating what to do.

Liston had previously shared with me a story of something that happened before he was two years old. He knew the story because his grandfather told it often.

One day, Little Liston was outside playing in the yard. Mr. Cherry was watching from the window, as the toddler was struggling to move an old tire. Liston would push and pull; observe the tire and its surroundings; then, work with the tire some more, trying his best to move that big tire that was more than twice his size. Little Liston never cried out in frustration nor yelled for help.

Mr. Cherry was inside the house secretly rooting for his grandson. "Looka dat boy. Look at him! He gon' move it. Watch. Look. Look at him!"

After a few minutes of toddler-determined force and strategy, that old tire lost its grip on its old resting place and began to move! Little Liston was moving that big old tire!

Proud Mr. Cherry was victorious right along with his only grandson! "I knew he was gon' move it! I knew he won't gon' give up, 'til it moved! Look at dat boy moving dat tire! Look at him!"

It was that same determination and leadership quality that led to Liston's becoming the youngest Yardmaster ever in New Jersey Transit's history at the age of 27; their first African American Yardmaster, and to beat his goal of purchasing his first house by the age of 30. He purchased at the age of 26!

This is the Liston who made the decision that Saturday to go out to that hot truck, in the middle-of-June, state-of-Virginia heat, undo item-by-item most of the packing that he had paid professional movers to do, and re-pack that truck to include the items the professional movers left out. What. A. MAN!

I kept him supplied with water and continually dried his face and head with a towel. By the time he finished, the sun had already set, and I was holding up a flashlight for him.

We decided to stay there one more night and get a few hours of sleep, so that Liston could get some much needed rest before driving that truck. We must have gotten a few items out of my car to make the floor as comfortable as possible. Maybe an air mattress was in my car and accessible.

The next morning was Sunday, June 16, 2013. We got an early start and drove the scenic route over the water which was the quickest and most-direct route. While we were on the road, he made sure I always drove in front of him, so he could watch over me. He had wanted to attach my car to the truck, so we could ride together. However, my car could not attach by the ball and joint equipment or whatever it's called. He would have had to use a different type of attachment on which my car would actually be sitting. I convinced him that paying all the extra money was not necessary, since the ride was only for five hours. I was used to the drive by that time, so he gave in. He really wanted us to ride together on the way to the rest of our lives as one. My Baby is just as sentimental as I am, if not more, and I absolutely love that about him!

"Sweetie, we are *driving* together into the rest of our lives as one!" I noted, hoping that was meaningful to him.

On our road to forever, there were so many thoughts in my mind and heart, as I reminisced about the divine alignment of our path together. I knew my husband was doing the same. Sometimes, we were on the phone together, as we drove, especially to share certain thoughts.

Finally, we turned into our subdivision; onto our street; then, into our driveway, and we were "Home, Sweet Home" in Willingboro, New Jersey! What a moment! We were cheesing like Cheshire cats with our hearts about to explode!

We were so glad to finally be permanently living together as man and wife, Mr. and Mrs. Clay L. Dowdy, in our own home, thirty-five years after we first met that summer of 1978!

First Christmas in our home! 2013

Timeline

June 1978	Liston and Arlene meet in Eastwood, NC
April 2008	The Grand Opening of Gaylord National
May 14, 2009	Arlene joins Facebook
June 29, 2009	Liston joins Facebook; searches for and finds Arlene and makes contact through an inbox message
Nov 2009	The debut of "Christmas on the Potomac" at Gaylord National
Dec 17, 2009	Liston greets Arlene for her birthday through an inbox message
Dec 17, 2010	Liston greets Arlene, who is in the Middle East, for her birthday through an inbox message
Dec 2011	Liston and Arlene are messaging more often
Dec 17, 2011	Liston greets Arlene for her birthday through an inbox message
March 2012	Liston and Arlene's first phone conversation since August 1978 and first time hearing each other's adult voices; the beginning of daily phone conversations
May 16, 2012	Liston and Arlene's face-to-face reunion; first time seeing each other since August 1978
June 28, 2012	Liston and Arlene, together in Burlington County, NJ
Aug 2, 2012	Liston visits Arlene for the 1st time, Newport News, VA
Sept 13, 2012	Liston proposes to Arlene; Arlene accepts; Liston and Arlene are engaged!
Oct 29, 2012	Hurricane Sandy brings devastation to New Jersey
Dec 15, 2012	Arlene meets Liston's family for the first time

Dr. Arlene Kearns Dowdy

Dec 17, 2012 Liston wishes Arlene "Happy Birthday" face to face for the very first time ever!

Dec 22, 2012 Liston meets Arlene's family

DECEMBER 25, 2012
LISTON AND ARLENE ARE MARRIED!

"Christmas on the Potomac"

at Gaylord National

APRIL 6, 2013
LISTON'S AND ARLENE'S PUBLIC, BIG WEDDING!

May 10, 2013 Liston & Arlene close on their house in Willingboro, NJ

JUNE 16, 2013
Liston & Arlene move into their Home, Sweet Home!

Sacred Secret Seed

Wedding Documents

December 25, 2012

An Intimate Evening Celebration of Endless Love

December 25, 2012　　　　　　　　　Gaylord National Resort
11:00 PM　　　　　　　　　　　　　　National Harbor, MD

Uniting
Arlene Kearns and Liston Dowdy
In Holy Matrimony

Opening Words and Prayer
Entrance of the Bride
The Vows
Exchange of Rings
Three-Fold Cord Ceremony
Prayer and Communion
Pronouncement of Marriage
Crowning Performance

Elder Shelton Sullivan, Officiating
Heavenly Designs and Creations, Photography
Karen Joseph, Special Soloist

Dr. Arlene Kearns Dowdy

April 6 2013

Arlene and Liston

Welcome Inside Our Hearts To

"A Celebration of Endless Love"

Saturday
April 6, 2013
3:00 PM

The Worship Center
150 Eastman Road
Southern Pines, NC

Officiators:

National Evangelist
Perry H. Hester,
Greensboro, NC

Pastor Sean Rajapakse,
Abu Dhabi, UAE

Wedding Directress:
Dr. Vanessa Alford,
Fayetteville, NC

Sacred Secret Seed

Pre-Wedding Video *"Our Endless Love"*

Song *"You Light Up My Life"* - Candle Lighting - Angels

Entrance of Bride's Mother
Entrance of Groom's Mother
Seating of Spiritual Mothers and Special Aunts
Seating of Honorary Bridesmaids

1 Corinthians 13 - Evangelist Ethelrine Hester and Dr. Gladys Long

"The Declaration of Ruth" – Ms. Dorothy Marsh

Words of Welcome – The Bride and Groom

Mime *"When the Saints Go to Worship"* - Ms. Fonda Barrett

Praise and Worship – Wedding Singers

Groom's Entrance

Ceremony Begins

Procession of the Wedding Party
"Make Us One" – Allison Boyke / *"Addictive Love"* – Prince Purcell and Lynda Wilson

Entrance of the Bride
"When God Made You" – Lavonia Cagle and DeAngelo Kearns

The Vows – The Ring – The Three-Fold Cord

Prayer of Blessings and Communion
Mime *"The Lord's Prayer"* – Mrs. Tameka Hester

Lighting of The Unity Candle
"A Love Like This" – Pastor Prince Purcell and Mrs. Lynda Wilson

Blessings and Pronouncement

Wedding Recession
"For Once in My Life" – Mrs. Ebony Walker

Dr. Arlene Kearns Dowdy

The Wedding Party

Matron of Honor
Sharonda B. Wilson – Niece "Daughter" of the Bride, Aberdeen, NC

Maid of Honor
Nancy Denise Smith – A Best Friend of the Bride, Anchorage, AK

Best Man
Steven Freeman – Military Buddy of the Groom, Wayne, NJ

Bridesmaids
Betanya Blake – Cousin of the Bride, Charlotte, NC
Eliza Diggs – Friend of the Bride, Pinehurst, NC
Tracy Jenyo – Friend of the Bride, Warri, Nigeria
Tonya Kearns – Eldest Niece of the Bride, Fayetteville, NC
Lisa McLean Rogers – Childhood Best Friend, Vass, NC
Lorraine McRae – Friend of the Bride, Newport News, VA
Paresi Newsome – Sister of the Groom, Newark, NJ
Jamala Akua Young – Friend "Daughter" of the Bride, Laurel, MD

Groomsmen
Ernest Brown – Military Buddy of the Groom, Buffalo, NY
Julian Caldwell – Friend of the Groom, Cedar Hill, TX
Aldwin Dishmey – Cousin of the Groom, Maplewood, NJ
Lindburg Gibbs – Military Buddy of the Groom, Little Rock, AR
Melvin Jones – A Friend of the Bride, Greensboro, NC
Moncello Marsh – Nephew and Godson of the Bride, Pinehurst, NC
Shawn Newsome – Nephew of the Groom, Newark, NJ
Michael Pratt – Cousin of the Groom, Newark, NJ

Junior Bridesmaids
Amber Gomez – Great Niece of the Bride, Pinehurst, NC
Angel Jackson – Goddaughter of the Bride, Pinehurst, NC
T'lasia Smaw – Great Niece of the Bride, Fayetteville, NC

Flower Girls
Arlena Wilson – Great Niece of the Bride, Aberdeen, NC
Heaven Wilson – Great Niece of the Bride, Aberdeen, NC

Ring Bearer
Zeldon Marsh – Great Nephew of the Bride, Southern Pines, NC

Sacred Secret Seed

Mother of the Groom
Palm Little

Father of the Groom
Clifton Little

Special Aunts
Dorothy Marsh
Christine McNair
Hawallion Wynn

Musicians
Pamela Bunch
Tryston Lawrence
Shawn McMillian
Tyrone McMillian

Wedding Singers
DeAngelo Kearns
(Nephew of the Bride)
Prince Purcell
Ebony Walker
(God-sister of the Bride)
Lynda Wilson
Goddaughters

Hostesses
Detri Cole
Antoinette Dukes
LaShell Laughlin
Glenice Woodard

Photography
Michael Woodard

Video
Ward Productions

Decorations:
Diane Potter

Mother of the Bride
Lillian Ruth Kearns

Eldest Uncle
Halbert Kearns

Spiritual Parents
Perry & Ethelrine Hester
Gladys Long

Honorary Bridesmaids
~Sisters~
Brenda K. Brown
Beverly Kearns
Blondell Kearns
Angela Kearns
Monique Fairley
Karim McArthur

~Goddaughters~
Allison Boyke
Kimberly Boyke
Lavonia Cagle
Benita Cagle
Freida Ford

Angel Trumpeteers
Rinardo Marsh
Phillip McArthur

Masters of the Aisle
Isaiah Cherry
Koreon Gillespie

Mimers
Fonda Barrett
Tameka Hester

A Memorial Candle will be lit in memory of Arlene's father, James Franklin Kearns, I.

The Three-Fold Cord Ceremony

Together, the bride and groom will tie three cords together to represent the bonding of their lives by and with the Holy Spirit, for "a three-fold cord is not easily broken". Marriage fuses two different people into one, so that under the pressures of life, they become so hard and fast that nothing can break them.

White

The white rope represents the purity, strength and power of the Holy Spirit.

Purple

Purple has power, a richness and quality that demand respect. Purple represents loyalty, luxury, ambition and self-assurance—the Leader, who is unique and individual, not one of the crowd, combining wisdom and power with sensitivity and humility.

Turquoise

Turquoise represents influence, open communication, clear thinking and decision-making. One who is usually self-sufficient, able to control the emotions, and to alleviate the feeling of loneliness. Turquoise represents peace, calm, tranquility and the enjoyment of life.

Releasing The Doves

~Doves choose one mate for life, and signify love and faithfulness. When they are separated for any length of time and then reunited, there is a joyous greeting when once again they are together. The white doves are a symbol of home building, teamwork, love, commitment, affection and lasting devotion.

~When they're in the cage together, doves spend a lot of time lovingly grooming each other and whispering their quiet cooing. Physical contact, not only lovemaking (though, of course, also lovemaking), is an important component to keeping the marriage vital.

~When doves leave the cage, it takes them a while to get their bearings, and then they head off in the same direction, but each on his or her own path. One person can't make a marriage. Marriage depends on the strength of the individuals to create a strong marriage. When the doves are released, it is a physical expression of the bride and groom starting a new life and facing the unknown together. Doves symbolize hope.

~Doves clearly enjoy the flight. The bride and groom commit to one another for the long haul, not only to the work and the struggle, but also to the fun and frivolity involved in sharing a life. Laughter and pleasure make the time fly by and give you resources for when life is difficult. The dove symbolizes joy.

*Releasing doves at the wedding is a sign of peace. Noah sent a dove out from the ark to make sure that the land was safe for humans to live on again after the flood. The dove is meant to be a symbol of peace in the couple's home and throughout their lives together.

Sacred Secret Seed

"A Heritage of Endless Love"
The Reception

Mr. and Mrs. Liston Dowdy

Director: Lucinda Dishmey

Guest Entrance Videos
~The Grand Entrance~
Parents
Honorees
The Wedding Party "Incwad'encane"

~The Royal Entrance~

Jumping the Broom

Best Man's Toast

Groom's Welcome and Invitation

Prayer and Blessing
~Pastors Samuel and Olivia Wright

~Dinner~

Maid of Honor's Toast and Musical Selections

Other Toasts
~The Father of the Groom, Cliff Little
~The Kearns Patriarch, Halbert Kearns
~Another Uncle of the Bride, Nathaniel Jackson

Remarks /Toasts by Others

A Special Nigerian Presentation ~ Olalekan and Tracy Jenyo

Gift- Giving

Cutting the Cake

Tossing the Bouquet

Tossing the Garter

The Royal Exit

~~~ ~~~ ~~~ ~~~ ~~~ ~~~

Reception Hosts: Justin Boyke   Samuel Brown
                    Keith Jackson   Ed Wilson

Cake: Wanda Gillespie

Incwad'encane by Zahara
(The wedding party's "Grand Entrance")

This is a song from the South African country of Zimbabwe.

<u>Translation:</u> One morning when I woke up, I saw a small letter. I saw that it was not from my mother, because if it were from her, she would have written, "Dear My Child." I continued reading this small letter. It was saying, "I don't know when I will come back, for I am embarking on my journey." I knew the letter was from the one I love.

Chorus: Where will I look? Who will I ask? ... I want to see the love of my life!

Biblical Reference: Song of Solomon 3:1-4, *By night on my bed I sought him whom my soul loveth: I sought him, but I found him not. I will rise now, and go about the city in the streets, and in the broad ways I will seek him whom my soul loveth: I sought him, but I found him not. The watchmen that go about the city found me: to whom I said, Saw ye him whom my soul loveth? It was but a little that I passed from them, but I found him whom my soul loveth: I held him, and would not let him go, until I had brought him into my mother's house, and into the chamber of her that conceived me.*

~Significance for us~

We were together as children. We went on our separate journeys,
One looking for the other—one fantasizing about the other.
As the wedding party turns, they're "looking around the world".
Now, dreams have become reality. Desires have been fulfilled.

Jumping the Broom
(For the Reception)

The broom ceremony should be practiced with honor for your ancestors and the beauty of our rich heritage. The significance of the broom to African American heritage and history dates back to the West African country of Ghana. In the 18th century, the Asante of The Ashanti Confederacy ruled most of Ghana. In Asante and other Akan cultures, the broom held spiritual value in addition to its home value. The broom symbolized the sweeping away of past wrongs or removing evil spirits. Brooms were waved over the heads of marrying couples to ward off spirits. The couple would often but not always jump over the broom at the end of the wedding ceremony, symbolizing the wife's commitment to the home and represented the determination of the one who ran the household. Jumping the broom was NOT a custom of slavery, as many Americans believe. Rather, it is a part of African culture that *survived* American slavery. Other African groups in the Americas learned the practice from slaves brought from the Asante area and used this practice to give legitimacy, dignity and strength to marriages in their communities during slavery.

Sacred Secret Seed

To Our Parents

Thank you for loving and encouraging us, for your wise leadership, and for your patience as you put up with us through the years. Because of your strong and powerful example, demonstrating to us the style of man and woman we should be in our lives, our lives have been a little easier.
We love you!

To Our Entire Wedding Party, Hosts and Hostesses

You have proven yourselves friends, "sisters" and "brothers". Thank you all for filling your place in our lives and for being the ones that we can always call on. You didn't hesitate to say, "Yes!" Thank you! All of you have that special place in our hearts that cannot be replaced by another. We love you!

To Our Musicians, Singers, Photographers, Etc.

Thank you for adding and capturing the joy, spirit, love, romance and overall ambience for our special day! You pressed through the difficulty of scattered distance between you to make this day special for us. Thank you for your part in my life for many, many years. We love you!

To Our Friends and Families

Oh my! You have definitely shown your love and care for us as you, too, prepared for this day! Thank you for being excited when you "heard the news" and for desiring to share in our excitement and happiness as we celebrate our union. You have come from far and near to be with us!
Believe this. We love YOU!

To God, Our Father and our Savior, Jesus Christ

Papa, You already know!! Whew! You planted this seed when we were just KIDS! Later in life, You led me into intercessory and warfare prayer for "my husband", when I didn't even know for whom I was praying! You caused him to hold on to the dream of being with me, when he thought it only a fantasy. THEN... THEN... more than 30 years later, when we were both fully ready for each other, you allowed Liston to find me.... Papa, Thank YOU!
YOU DID THIS THANG!! And, WE LOVE YOU!!

Dr. Arlene Kearns Dowdy

About the Author

Dr. Arlene Kearns Dowdy has a doctoral degree in Missions and Evangelism and has been a teacher and evangelist for more than thirty years. She has ministered in many parts of the United States as well as more than 15 other countries and islands and has been a teacher and leader in public schools since 1985.

An international traveler, Dr. Dowdy has a passion for the welfare of all people. She lives her life helping others and has learned that people have the same needs wherever you go. To inspire and encourage the fulfillment of those needs, Dr. Dowdy shares her faith and speaks the oracles of God.

Raised in the church and in prayer, Dr. Dowdy is a firm believer of Jesus Christ. This is the faith that kept her single and saved throughout her teenage, high school, college and young adult years so that she would be available for her miracle of Clay Liston Dowdy!

Dr. Dowdy finally married at the age of 50! Christmas night of 2012, Arlene married Liston, a childhood sweetheart, who found her after 31 years! Dr. Dowdy now resides in South Jersey, writing her poems, books and stories and helping others to become authors by writing their own stories.

Join Dr. Dowdy in *"**Breakthrough Prayer!**"*
Each **Wednesday** morning,
5:30 a.m. EST – 6:30 a.m.
Call: 1-712-770-8004
Code: 111879

Other Books by This Author

Tales of Eastwood

More Tales of Eastwood

There is Purpose in Your Valley

My Name is Miss Katydid

Lake of the Swans

For Our Children Our Future

Out of Her Belly: A Poetry Collection

Wisdom and Pineal Series: Wanna Know a Secret?

www.ingramcontent.com/pod-product-compliance
Lightning Source LLC
LaVergne TN
LVHW051601070426
835507LV00021B/2708